PROOFREADERS' MARKS

$\smile$	close up space
$\mathcal{S}$	delete
$\underset{\smile}{\mathcal{S}}$	delete and close up space
#	separate with a space
$\wedge$	insert here what is indicated in the margin
¶	start new paragraph
no ¶	no paragraph; run in with previous paragraph
$\odot/$	insert period
$\overset{\wedge}{,}/$	insert comma
$;/$	insert semicolon
$:/$	insert colon
$\frac{1}{M}/$	insert em dash
$\frac{1}{M}/\frac{1}{M}$	insert pair of em dashes
$=/$	insert hyphen
$\overset{\vee}{\,}/$	insert apostrophe
(cap)	use capital letter here
(lc)	use lowercase letter here
$(ital)$	set in italic type
(rom)	set in roman type
(sc)	set in small capitals
(bf)	set in boldface type
(tr)	transpose letters or words

The Little English Handbook: Choices and Conventions

Second Edition

Edward P. J. Corbett
The Ohio State University

John Wiley & Sons, Inc.
New York / Santa Barbara / London / Sydney / Toronto

This book was set in Helvetica Light by York Graphic Services, Inc., and printed and bound by Murray Printing. Editor: Arthur Vergara. Designer: Eileen Thaxton. Production Manager: Suzanne Ingrao. Cover by Eileen Thaxton.

Library of Congress Cataloging in Publication Data

Corbett, Edward P J
The little English handbook.

Includes index.
1. English language—Rhetoric. I. Title.
PE1408.C587   1977   808'.042   76-27339
ISBN 0-471-17229-4

Printed in the United States of America

10 9 8 7 6

This book is dedicated to all my students over the years, whose written prose sometimes mystified me, often enlightened me, and invariably beguiled me. Bless them all.

Preface to Second Edition

The idea of a little handbook seems to have appealed to a great number of teachers and students. Users of a little handbook must be willing, of course, to forgo many of the features available in comprehensive handbooks, and apparently they have been. A constant refrain from those who wrote to me or buttonholed me at meetings, even from those who suggested features that might be added, has been, "Keep the little handbook little."

Nothing that was in the first edition has been dropped, but a few additions and changes have been made. A new item **(90)** on capitalization has been added to the mechanics section. Item **40** has been expanded to include a discussion of faulty predication. Item **62,** which deals with the omission of the comma in pairs of words, phrases, and dependent clauses joined by a coordinating conjunction, has been expanded to include an exception to that convention in the case of "suspended constructions." Item **89** (about numbers) has been expanded to include more than merely the rule not to begin a sentence with an Arabic number. A complete paradigm of the tenses of regular and irregular verbs and the verb *to be* has been added in an unnumbered section at the back of the book. A list of the official two-letter

Preface

postal abbreviations of all the states has also been added at the back of the book. A sample of a business letter typed on letterhead stationery and a complete termpaper, instead of just a few sample pages, have been added to this edition. Although I adhered to my original decision not to include a Glossary of Usage, I did add a brief section of Puzzlers, which deals with some common problems of phrasing. In response to requests from many users, I have provided a system of reference to the research-paper section by using letters of the alphabet. Throughout the book I have added or substituted new examples wherever the previous examples did not seem to cover all the varieties of error, and here and there, I have revised some of my inanities.

Although these additions and changes have made the handbook slightly larger, I hope that you will still think of it as being "little."

Edward P. J. Corbett

Preface to First Edition

This handbook is designed to serve as a guide on basic matters of grammar, style, paragraphing, punctuation, and mechanics for those engaged in writing public prose. By "public prose" is meant that dialect of written English most commonly used in the newspapers, magazines, and books that the majority of educated native speakers read. This ranges in style from the formal to the casual, from the literary to the colloquial. But because public prose seeks to be intelligible to a general audience, it avoids the strictly in-group vocabulary of various professional, regional, and social groups, and it observes the rules of grammar as taught in the schools.

The use of this term is not intended to disparage the other current dialects, most of which serve well the needs of some of the people all of the time and all of the people some of the time. Obviously, spoken English, with its own wide range of professional, regional, and social dialects, serves the needs of more people more often than written English does. In fact, many people speak more words in a single week than they will write during a lifetime. When linguists say that the spoken language is the primary language, they mean that the spoken comes first in point of time (centuries before the written form

Preface

developed) and use (in a single lifetime, before the written language is learned). Also, more natives have a command of the spoken language than have a command of both the spoken and the written. However, despite the primacy of the spoken language, there are occasions when many, if not most, native speakers must use the written language in order to record or communicate their thoughts, needs, and feelings. It is for those occasions that this handbook is designed.

When a person wishes to communicate in the written medium, it is natural for him to resort—or wish that he could resort—to a more sophisticated style of language than the one he is accustomed to use in the conduct of his everyday affairs. Actually, in his first fumbling efforts at writing, he might succeed better if he used the lexical and syntactical resources acquired from daily practice in the oral medium. But as the written transcription of impromptu talk reveals, the spoken language is often marked by redundancy of language, imprecision of diction, and loose, rambling, dislocated sentence patterns. Words and structures that may have communicated adequately in the oral medium because of the aid furnished by voice and gesture are something less than adequate when inscribed on paper. For effective written communication, words must be more precise, structures tighter, and organization more discernible; and graphic devices of punctuation and mechanics must be relied on to do what the intonation of the voice does in the oral medium. The kind of public prose used by newscasters on television and radio and by writers in newspapers, magazines, and books has proven to be the most efficient medium for communicating on paper with a general audience.

In this little handbook, I concentrate on those matters of grammar, style, paragraphing, punctuation, and mechanics that from years of experience in reading student papers and responding to telephone queries from businessmen and secretaries I know to be the most common and persistent problems in the expressive part of the writing process. For answers to the larger or more subtle problems in writing prose, you will have to consult one of the comprehensive rhetoric handbooks that are readily available. I do not, for instance, provide guidance in all the uses of the comma; some of these are never or seldom a problem for writers. Instead, I deal only with those half-dozen conventions of the comma that are most often ignored or misused and that are most crucial for the preservation of clarity. If you master these six, you can rest assured that there are no really serious mistakes that you can make in the use (or omission) of the comma.

Nor does this handbook carry a section that is a common feature of comprehensive handbooks, a glossary of usage. Although questions of usage—whether to use *contact* as a verb, the conjunction *like* or *as,* the preposition *due to* or *because of,* the construction *different than* or *different from* —are troublesome problems, a glossary of usage has been excluded from this handbook for two reasons: (1) to be really useful, it would have to be at least thirty pages long, which would make this a bigger book than I wanted, and (2) even if I knew more than I do about the current status of certain locutions, I would find it difficult to make pronouncements about questions of usage outside the norm of a context. If the writer has a question about usage, he can consult one of the book-length authorities, such as H. W. Fowler's *A Dictionary of Modern English Usage,* Bergen and Cornelia Evans's *A Dictionary of Contemporary American Usage,* or Wilson Follett's *Modern American Usage.*

Preface

The subtitle of this handbook, *Choices and Conventions,* reflects my approach to the matters I deal with. Some of the principles governing the system of writing have been established by convention; others represent a recommendation from a number of available options. Accordingly, in most cases, I have stated the guiding principle in definite, unequivocal terms. It should quickly be added, however, that there are no absolute prescriptions in matters of language. Where choices are available, a selection must be guided by a consideration of the subject matter, occasion, desired effect, and audience. But in my experience, the kind of person who needs the guidance of a handbook like this wants a simple, straightforward answer to his query—e.g. "How do I punctuate this compound sentence?" He does not yet have enough sophistication in the use of the written language to be much helped by the advice, "In most cases, you should separate the two clauses of a compound sentence with a comma, but often when the clauses are short, you can dispense with the comma without any loss of clarity." Such a person is better served if he is told that he should *always* put a comma in front of the coordinating conjunction that joins the two independent clauses of a compound sentence. There is also a practical value attaching to the unequivocal advice: rarely will the writer go wrong if he follows it, but he may expect to go wrong on occasion if he ignores it.

It is assumed that the user of this handbook has acquired at least a basic knowledge of formal grammar and that the grammatical system to which he has most likely been exposed is the "traditional" one. Thus when such terms as *compound sentence, independent clause, participial phrase* are used, the writer will probably be able to recognize the structures to which the terms refer. Also, the diagram of structures that accompanies many of the statements of principle will serve as a visual aid for those whose knowledge of traditional terminology has faded and for those whose training has been predominantly in structural grammar or in transformational-generative grammar. Thus, the "picture" of a structure will usually be a sufficient guide for those who are impatient with, or are baffled by, technical terminology. However, to ensure maximum comprehension, I have furnished the book with a glossary of grammatical terms.

About 90 percent of the examples—both those that illustrate the observance of the principle and those that illustrate the violation of it—have been taken directly from student writing. A few examples had to be invented, but even these are typical of sentences that students write. In the case of those examples that illustrate violations of the principle, no ridicule of the writer is intended. I simply want to exhibit, from prose written in the 1970s, examples of aberrations from the prevailing conventions. In the explanatory matter that follows the examples, I frequently show why the aberration is a threat to clear communication and how it might be corrected.

By concentrating on matters of grammar, style, paragraphing, punctuation, and mechanics, I do not wish to imply that these are the most important concerns of "good writing." What is most essential for effective communication is the substance, originality, and sophistication of one's thoughts and the ability to organize them in a unified, coherent way. However, sloppy articulation of one's thoughts is often a reflection of sloppy inventional and organizational processes; it is easily demonstrable that careless expression stems ultimately from careless thinking. Observance of the "basics" treated in this handbook will not guarantee that your prose will be interesting or worth reading, but observance of the fundamental conventions of the writing system will at least guarantee that your prose *can* be read. Readable prose is no mean achievement. The next achievement to strive for is to write prose that others will *want* to read.

Edward P. J. Corbett

Acknowledgments

Every textbook designed for the classroom profits from the criticisms and suggestions of experienced, knowledgeable teachers. I profited immensely from the criticisms and suggestions of those who reviewed the manuscript of the first edition: James T. Nardin of Louisiana State University, Gary Tate of Texas Christian University, William F. Irmscher of the University of Washington, James Karabatsos of Creighton University, Marinus Swets of Grand Rapids Junior College, Richard Lloyd-Jones of the University of Iowa, Mina P. Shaughnessy of City College of the City University of New York, Kirby L. Duncan of Stephen F. Austin University, Nancy Dasher of Ohio State University, Betty Renshaw of Prince George's Community College, and Raymond D. Liedlich of Portland Community College. For the second edition, I can acknowledge only in a general way my debt to the legion of teachers and students who passed on to me, either in person or in letters, their criticisms and encouragement. I owe a special debt, however, to the following people who gave me detailed suggestions for improving the book: W. G. Schermbrucker of Capilano College in North Vancouver, B.C., Maureen Waters Oser of Queens College in New York, Sarah M. Wallace and her colleagues at Volunteer Community Col-

Acknowledgments

lege in Tennessee, Peter T. Zoller of Wichita State University, Robert C. Fox of St. Francis College, James T. Nardin of Louisiana State University, Paul Sorrentino of the Pennsylvania State University, and Nancy Bandez of John Wiley and Sons.

I am heavily indebted to the editorial and production staff at John Wiley, especially to Thomas O. Gay and Arthur Vergara. I am indebted also to those standard handbooks and meticulously edited magazines that have instructed me all these years about the choices and conventions of written English. The errors and shortcomings of the book should be attributed solely to me.

E.P.J.C.

Note to the Writer

You are fortunate if you have an instructor or an editor or a knowledgeable friend who will read what you have written and call attention to the strengths and weaknesses of your prose by writing comments in the margin or at the end of your paper. Comments of that sort, especially when they are judicious and constructive, can be of great help to you in improving your writing. You should value those personal notes, and whenever the correction, question, suggestion, praise, or blame in them strikes you as being well grounded, you would do well to heed it.

To call attention, however, to routine matters of grammar, style, paragraphing, punctuation, or mechanics, your accommodating critic may resort to some kind of shorthand notations. If he knows that you have a copy of this handbook, he may underline or encircle something in your manuscript and write a number in the margin. If, for instance, he scribbles the number 83 in the margin, he is suggesting that you look at item **83** in the section on mechanics. Turning to this item in the handbook, you will find that it has to do with italicizing certain kinds of titles. Perhaps you failed to italicize the title of a book you mentioned, or perhaps instead of italicizing the title of the book, you enclosed it in quotation

Note to the Writer

marks. The principle stated opposite the number **83** may be all that you need to read. But if you need further enlightenment about what you have done wrong, you can look at the graphic diagram of the structure involved (if one is presented for that principle) or at the examples printed below the principle, or you can go on to read the explanation of the principle.

For more complicated matters, the explanation in the handbook may not be sufficient to point out what you have done wrong or to prevent you from making the mistake again. If so, you should arrange to have a conference with the critic of your prose. Although the correction symbols in the margin may strike you as being heartlessly impersonal, it would be a mistake for you to regard them as petulant slaps on the wrist. They are intended to help you discover how to put your written prose in the ''proper'' form.

This handbook is also intended to serve as a guide to the writer who does not have an instructor or a friend to read and criticize what he has written. Usually, once a writer has completed a Freshman English course or an advanced composition course of some kind, he no longer enjoys the advantage of frequent, expert criticism of his prose. (If he does, he probably has to pay for the service.) If kept at hand, along with such other reference books as a dictionary and a thesaurus, this handbook can be a useful guide for the writer when he sits down to write something that he wants others to read. The reference charts on the endpages will direct him to the section that deals with his particular problem of the moment. For example, ''Should the modifying clause in this sentence be enclosed with commas?'' Somewhere in its pages, the handbook probably provides a straightforward answer to that query.

Contents

Contents

Contents

Contents

Format of Research Paper

Forms for Letters

Legend

Some of the principles, especially those having to do with punctuation, are illustrated with graphic models, using these symbols:

$$\boxed{} = \text{word}$$

A word inside the box designates a particular part of speech, e.g. $\boxed{\text{NOUN}}$

$$\underline{} = \text{phrase}$$

The following abbreviations on the horizontal line designate a particular kind of phrase, e.g. $\underline{\text{PREP.}}$:

prep. = prepositional phrase **(on the stagecoach).**
part. = participial phrase **(having ridden on the stage-coach).**
ger. = gerund phrase (**riding on the stagecoach** pleased him).

Legend

inf. = infinitive phrase (he wanted **to ride on the stage-coach**).

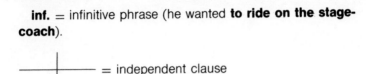 = independent clause

An independent clause, sometimes referred to as a "main clause," can stand by itself as a grammatically complete sentence, e.g. **He rode on the stagecoach.**

 = dependent clause

A dependent clause cannot stand by itself as a grammatically complete sentence. The following abbreviations printed above the first vertical line designate a particular kind of dependent clause, e.g. noun.

 :

noun = noun clause (He claimed **that he rode on the stagecoach**).
adj. = adjective clause (The man **who rode on the stagecoach** was pleased).
adv. = adverb clause (He was late **because he rode on the stagecoach**).

Format of Manuscript

In preparing the final draft of a manuscript, follow the specific directions about format given by your instructor or editor. However, if no specific directions are given, you can be confident that the format of your manuscript will be acceptable if you observe the following conventions:

10
Write on one side of the paper only.

11
Double-space the lines of prose, whether you handwrite or typewrite.

A manuscript submitted to an editor for consideration must be typewritten and double-spaced.

Format of Manuscript

12

Preserve a left-hand and a right-hand margin.

On the left-hand side, leave at least a 1½-inch margin. On the right-hand side, try to preserve about a 1-inch margin. If you are handwriting your manuscript on theme paper, the vertical red line will set your left-hand margin. Try to leave an inch of space between the last line and the bottom edge of the page.

13

Put the title of your paper at the top of the first page of your manuscript—even though you may have put the title on a cover sheet.

See **84** for instructions about how to set down the title of your paper.

14

Number all pages, after the first one, at the top of the page—either in the middle or at the right-hand margin.

Be sure to assemble the pages of your manuscript in the right sequence.

15

Secure your manuscript with a paper clip—*never* with a staple or pin.

Many editors will not even read a manuscript that is stapled together.

16
Use the proper kind of paper.

If you typewrite your manuscript, use white, unlined, opaque paper. If you handwrite your manuscript, use white, lined theme paper. Never submit a formal written assignment on pages torn from a spiral notebook.

Grammar

Grammar may be defined as the study of how a language "works"—a study of how the structural system of a language combines with a vocabulary to convey meaning. When we study a foreign language in school, we must study both **vocabulary** and **grammar,** and until we can put the two together, we cannot translate the language. Sometimes we know the meaning of every word in a foreign-language sentence, and yet we cannot translate the sentence because we cannot figure out its grammar. On the other hand, we sometimes can figure out the syntax of the foreign-language sentence, but because we do not know the meaning of one or more words in the sentence, we still cannot translate the sentence.

If a native speaker of English heard or read this sequence of words

> The porturbs in the brigger torms have tanted the makrets' rotment brokly.

he would perceive that the sequence bears a marked resemblance to an English sentence. Although many words in that sequence would be unfamiliar to him, he would detect that the sequence had the structure of the kind of English sentence that makes a statement, and he might further surmise that this kind of statement pattern was one that said that *porturbs* (whoever they are) had done something to *rotment* (whatever that is), or, to put it another way, that *porturbs* was the subject of the sentence, that *have tanted* was the predicate verb (transitive), and that *rotment* was the object of that transitive verb, the receiver of the action performed by the doer, *porturbs*. How was he able to make that much ''sense'' out of that sequence of strange words? He was able to detect that much ''sense'' by noting the following structural signals:

☐ Function words:

The three occurrences of the article **the;** the preposition **in;** and the auxiliary verb **have.**

☐ Inflections and affixes:

The **-s** added to nouns to form the plural; the **-er** added to adjectives to form the comparative degree; the **-ed** added to verbs to form the past tense or the past participle; the **-s'** added to nouns to form the plural possessive case; the affix **-ment** added to certain words to form an abstract noun; and the **-ly** added to adjectives to form adverbs.

☐ Word order:

The basic pattern of a statement or declarative sentence in English is S (subject) + V (verb) + C (complement) or NP (noun phrase) + VP (verb phrase). In the sequence, **The porturbs in the brigger torms** appears to be the S or NP part of the sentence and **have tanted the makrets' rotment brokly** the VP part of the sentence (**have tanted** being the V and **the makrets' rotment brokly** being the C).

☐ Intonation (stress, pitch, terminals, and juncture):

If the sequence were spoken aloud, the native speaker would detect that the sequence had the intonational pattern of a declarative sentence in spoken English.

Grammar

☐ **Punctuation and mechanics:**

   If the sequence were written out (as it is here), the native speaker would observe that the sequence began with a capital letter and ended with a period, two typographical devices that signal a statement in written English.

The native speaker of English has been able to read all of this meaning into the string of nonsense words simply by observing the *grammatical* devices of **inflections, function words, word order,** and **intonation** (if spoken) or **punctuation** (if written). Now, if he had a dictionary that defined such words as *porturb, brig, torm, tant, makret, rotment,* and *brok,* he would be able to translate the full meaning of the sentence. But by observing the structural or grammatical devices alone, the native speaker of English has perceived that the sequence of words

   The porturbs in the brigger torms have tanted the makrets' rotment brokly.

exactly matches the structure of an English sentence like this one:

   The citizens in the larger towns have accepted the legislators' commitment enthusiastically.

What he has been concentrating on is the *grammar* of the sentence, and it is in this sense that we use the term *grammar* in the section that follows.

   Almost every child has mastered the fundamentals of this grammatical system of English by the time he starts school. He has "mastered grammar" in the sense that he can form original and meaningful English sentences of his own and can understand English sentences uttered by others. He may not "know grammar" in the sense that he can analyze the structure of sentences and label the parts, but he knows grammar in the sense that he can *perform appropriately* in the language—that is, that he can utter and respond to properly formed sentences.

In a sense, the grammar of a language is a convention. We formulate sentences in a certain way because communities of native speakers of the language, over a long period of time, have developed, and agreed on, certain ways of saying something. The grammar of a language allows some choices but proscribes others. For instance, if you wanted to tell someone that a certain boy kissed a certain girl in a certain manner, grammar would allow you one of these choices of patterns:

> The boy kissed the girl passionately.
> The boy passionately kissed the girl.
> Passionately the boy kissed the girl.
> The girl was kissed passionately by the boy.

Grammar would not allow you to use one of these patterns:

> The girl kissed the boy passionately.
>
> (*this is a grammatical sentence, but because of the altered word order, it does not say what you wanted it to say. Here the girl is the doer of the action, and the boy is the receiver of the action*)
>
> The passionately boy the girl kissed.
> Kissed boy the passionately girl the.

The choice of which grammatically acceptable pattern a writer will use is a concern of style, which will be dealt with in the next section.

In this section on grammar, we are dealing with those devices of *inflection, function words,* and *word order* that

Grammar

must be observed if written sentences are to convey the intended meaning to a reader clearly and unequivocally. We do not deal in this section with *intonation,* because this handbook is concerned only with the written language. In a later section of this handbook, we shall deal with the fourth grammatical device of written English, *punctuation.*

20

Use an apostrophe for the possessive, or genitive, case of the noun.

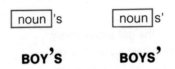

Here are some guidelines on forming the possessive, or genitive, case of the English noun:

(a) As indicated in the diagrams above, most English nouns form the possessive case with **'s** (singular) or **s'** (plural). (An alternative form of the genitive consists of an **of** phrase: **the general's commands** or **the commands of the general**.)

(b) The possessive case of nouns that form their plural in ways other than by adding an **s** is formed by adding **'s** to the plural of the noun: **man's/men's, woman's/women's, child's/children's, ox's/oxen's, deer's/deer's, mouse's/mice's.**

(c) Some writers simply add an apostrophe to form the possessive case of nouns ending in **s:**

the actress' fame

the alumnus' contribution

Keats' odes

Dickens' death

However, other writers add the usual **'s** to form the possessive case of such nouns: **actress's, alumnus's** (plural, **alumni's**), **Keats's, Dickens's.** Take your choice, but be consistent.

(d) The rules for forming the possessive case of pairs of nouns are as follows: (1) in the case of joint possession, add **'s** only to the second member of the pair: **John and Mary's mother, the brother and sister's car,** and (2) in the case of individual possession, add **'s** to each member of the pair: **the boy's and girl's bedrooms, John's and Mary's tennis rackets, the men's and women's locker rooms.**

(e) Form the possessive case of group nouns and compound nouns by adding **'s** to the end of the unit: **commander in chief's, someone else's, president-elect's, editor in chief's, son-in-law's.** In the case of those compounds that form their plural by adding **s** to the first word, form the plural possessive case by adding **'s** to the end of the unit: **editors in chief's, sons-in-law's.**

(f) Normally the **'s** or **s'** is reserved for the genitive case of nouns naming animate creatures (human beings and animals). The **of** phrase is commonly used for the genitive case of inanimate nouns: not **the house's roof** but **the roof of the house.** Usage, however, now sanctions the use of **'s** with a number of inanimate nouns: **a day's wages, a week's work, the year's death toll, the school's policies, the car's performance, the radio's tone.**

Grammar

21

**Its is the possessive case of the pronoun it;
it's is the contraction of it is or it has.**

More mistakes have been made with the pronoun **it** than with any other single word in the English language. The mistakes result from confusion about the two **s** forms of this pronoun. **It's** is used where **its** is the correct form **(The dog broke it's leg** instead of **The dog broke its leg), and its** is used where **it's** is the correct form **(Its a shame that the girl broke her leg** instead of **It's a shame that the girl broke her leg).**

The writer who uses **it's** for the possessive case of **it** is probably influenced by the **'s** that is used to form the possessive case of the singular noun **(man's hat).** He might be helped to avoid this mistake if he would remember that none of the personal pronouns uses **'s** to form its possessive case: **I/my, you/your, he/his, she/her, it/its, we/our, they/their.** So he should write, **The company lost its lease.**

Or the writer might be helped to avoid this mistake if he would remember that the apostrophe has another function in written English: to indicate the omission of one or more letters in an English word, as in contractions **(I'll, don't, he'd).** The apostrophe in the word **it's** signals the contraction of the expression **it is** or **it has.** So he should write, **It's the first loss the company has suffered** or **It's come to my attention that you are frequently late.**

Don't let this little word defeat you. Get **it** right, once and for all.

22

The predicate verb should agree in number with its subject.

SINGULAR NOUN OR PRONOUN	SINGULAR FORM OF VERB
NOUN (no S) boy	VERB S runS

PLURAL NOUN OR PRONOUN	PLURAL FORM OF VERB
NOUN S boyS	VERB (no S) run

In addition to these differentiated forms of the verb in the third person, present tense, we have to be concerned about the few differentiated forms of the verb **to be (am/is/are; was/were)** and of auxiliary verbs **(has/have; does/do).**

The English verb has been evolving toward a single form for the singular and plural of all three persons (first, second, third)—as witness the **-ed** ending added to the verb in all three persons, singular and plural, of the past tense—and we may yet live to see the day when a totally simplified form of the English verb is achieved. In the meanwhile, the few remaining

Grammar

differentiated forms of the verb will probably continue to give writers some trouble.

Some typical examples of faulty agreement:

1 He **don't** care about anything.
2 The lawyer and his client **agrees** on a fee.
3 If any one of the substations **are knocked** out, we can resort to reserve stations.
4 The jury **has** made up **their** minds.
5 He finds it impossible to live with the ignorance, injustice, poverty, and prejudice that **surrounds** him.
6 Neither the gambler nor Jake **are** really bitter about their bad luck or **blame** anyone for their misfortunes.

Expressions like **He don't care about anything** are not so much "mistakes" in agreement as carry-overs from the dialect that a person speaks, quite acceptably, in his community. Such a person should be made aware of the standard form of the verb in written prose: **He doesn't care about anything** (a singular verb with a singular subject).

Most errors of agreement in written prose are the result of carelessness, inadvertence, or uncertainty. The writer often knows better; he merely slips up. Errors in agreement often occur when several words intervene between the simple subject of the sentence and the predicate verb, as in our third example above: **If any one of the substations are knocked out.** . . . The simple subject of the **if** clause here is **one,** but because the plural noun **substations** (the object of the preposition **of**) intervened between that singular subject and the verb, the writer was influenced to use the plural form of the verb **(are knocked out)** instead of the correct singular form **(is knocked out).** Careful proofreading will often catch such inadvertent errors of agreement.

Errors due to uncertainty are another matter. Uncertainty

about whether the verb should be singular or plural arises in cases where (1) the subject is compound; (2) the subject is a collective noun; (3) the subject of the sentence follows the expletive structure **there is** or **there are;** and (4) the subject takes the form of structures like **one of those who** and **this man as well as.** Here are some guidelines for these puzzling cases:

(a) Compound subject

(1) Singular subjects joined by **and** usually take a plural verb.

John and his sister **were questioned** by the police.

(2) Singular subjects joined by **or** or by the correlative conjunctions **either . . . or, neither . . . nor** take a singular verb.

John or his sister **runs** the store during the week.

Neither the gambler nor Jake **is** really bitter about his bad luck or **blames** anyone for his misfortunes.

(3) When both subjects are plural, the verb is plural.

The detectives and the insurance agents **have expressed** their belief in the innocence of the brother and sister.

Neither the detectives nor the insurance agents **have expressed** any doubts about the innocence of the brother and sister.

(4) When one subject is singular and the other subject is plural and the subjects are joined by **or** or by the correlative conjunctions **either . . . or, neither . . . nor, both . . . and, not only . . . but also,** the verb agrees in number with the closest subject.

15

Grammar

Either John or his parents **have agreed** to cooperate with the police.

Neither the brothers nor the sister **appears** to be cooperative.

(b) Collective noun as subject

(1) If the collective noun is considered as a **group,** the verb is singular.

The jury **has made up** its mind.

The committee **was elected** unanimously.

The number of students drafted last month **was increased** by 50 percent.

(2) If the collective noun is considered as **individuals** of a group, each acting on his own, the verb is plural.

The jury **have made up** their minds.

The committee **wish** to offer their congratulations to the new chairman.

A number of students **have petitioned** the draft board for a deferment.

(c) Expletive structure **there is/was, there was/were**

(1) If the delayed or real subject following the expletive **there** is singular, the verb is singular.

There **is** a remarkable consensus among the committee members.

(2) If the delayed or real subject following the expletive **there** is plural, the verb is plural.

There **were** ten dissenting votes from the stockholders.

(d) Special structures

(1) In the structure **one of the** (plural noun) **who,** the predicate verb of the **who** clause is plural, because the antecedent of the subject **who** is the plural noun rather than the singular **one.**

> Matilda is one of the women who **refuse** to accept the ruling.
>
> (*here the antecedent of **who** is the plural noun **women***)

(2) Exception: if **the only** precedes **one of the** (plural noun) **who,** the predicate verb of the **who** clause is singular, because the subject **who** in that case refers to the singular **one** rather than to the plural object of the preposition **of.**

> Matilda is the only one of the women who **refuses** to accept the ruling.

(3) A singular subject followed by structures like **as well as, in addition to, together with** takes a singular verb.

(A plural subject, of course, followed by any of these structures, would take a plural verb. See the third example below.)

> The sergeant as well as his superior officers **praises** his platoon.
>
> Gill Dougal along with his roommate **has denied** the charges.
>
> The students together with their counselor **deny** that there has been any distribution of hash in the dorms.

23

A pronoun must agree in person, number, and gender with its antecedent noun.

17

Grammar

Examples of faulty agreement between a pronoun and its antecedent:

1 A **family** cannot go camping these days without a truckload of gadgets to make **your** campsite look just like home.
2 The crew threw some floatable **items** overboard for the sailor, even though they knew that **it** would probably not save him.
3 The **university** did not live up to **his** promise to the students.

Pronouns, which are substitutes for nouns, have, in common with nouns, **number** (singular and plural) and **gender** (masculine, feminine, and neuter). What nouns and pronouns do not share in common is the full range of **person.** All nouns are **third person** exclusively; but some pronouns are **first person (I, we),** some are **second person (you),** and some are **third person (e.g. he, she, it, they, one, some, none, all).**

A firm grammatical principle is that a pronoun must correspond with whatever of those three aspects of person, number, and gender it shares with its antecedent noun. A second-person pronoun cannot be linked with a third-person noun (see the first example above); a singular pronoun cannot be linked with a plural noun (see the second example above); a masculine pronoun cannot be linked with a neuter noun (see the third example above).

Simple as the grammatical principle is that governs the relationship of a pronoun with its antecedent, there are a few tricky problems for the writer in making a pronoun agree in person, number, and gender with its noun. For one thing, the English language has no convenient pronoun for indicating masculine-*or*-feminine gender. When a noun could be either masculine or feminine, a writer is tempted to use an awkward pronoun form like **his or her, his/her,** or **his (her),** as in the following sentence: "The student should bring **his or her** schedule cards to the bursar's office.'' One way around that awkward locution is to use a plural noun: "**Students** should bring **their** schedule cards to the bursar's office." Another way is to settle for one gender in the pronoun, with the implication that the other sex is included in the reference if applicable: "The student should bring **his** schedule cards to the bursar's office."

Another problem stems from the ambiguity of **number** of such pronouns as **everyone, everybody, all, none, some, each.** Although there are exceptions, the following guidelines are generally reliable:

(a) Everyone, everybody, anybody, anyone invariably take singular verbs and, in formal usage at least, should be referred to by a singular pronoun.

Everyone brings **his** schedule cards to the bursar's office. (*formal usage*)

Everyone brings **their** schedule cars to the bursar's office. (*informal usage*)

(b) All and **some** are singular *or* plural according to the context. If the **of** phrase following the pronoun specifies a *mass* or *bulk* of something, the pronoun is singular; if the **of** phrase specifies a *number of things or persons,* the pronoun is plural.

Some of the fabric lost **its** coloring.

Some of the young men turned in **their** draft cards.

All of the draftees registered **their** complaints about the exemption procedure.

(c) None is singular or plural according to the context (the distinction in particular cases is sometimes so subtle that a writer could justify either one).

Grammar

None of the young men **was** willing to turn in **his** draft card. (*but* **were . . . their** *could also be justified in this case*)

None of the young men in the hall **were** as tall as **their** fathers. (*here it would be harder to justify the singular forms* **was . . . his**)

(d) **Each** is almost invariably singular.

Each of them declared **his** allegiance to democracy.

If you match up your pronouns in person, number, and gender with their antecedent nouns, you will make it easier for your reader to figure out what the pronouns refer to.

24

A pronoun should have a clear antecedent.

? · · · · | PRONOUN |

Examples of no antecedent or an unclear antecedent for the pronoun:

1 He retraced his steps to the bedroom, but **it** appeared to be hopeless.

(*what appeared to be hopeless?*)

2 John told his father that **his** car wouldn't start.

(*whose car? the father's or John's?*)

3 The word **deer** originally meant a wild animal, **which** first appeared in the twelfth century.

(*what first appeared in the twelfth century? the word* **deer?** *a wild animal? or* **meaning?**—*a word that is not in the previous clause*)

4 The league's first major step was to sponsor a cleanup day, but **it** could not enlist enough volunteers.

(*a pronoun should not refer to a noun functioning as a posses-sive or as a modifier—here **league's***)

5 He is a strictly passive character, buffeted by fate, driven hither and yon, the unwilling pawn of forces stronger than himself. **This** makes him resent all offers of help.

(***this** refers to an idea or a situation in the previous sentence, not to some noun in that sentence; but it is not even clear **which** idea or situation is being referred to*)

Careless handling of the pronoun often blocks communica-tion between a writer and his reader. The writer always knows what he meant the pronoun to stand for, but if there is no noun in the previous group of words to which the pronoun can refer, or if it is difficult to find the noun to which the pronoun refers, the reader will not know—and will have to guess—what the pronoun stands for.

A good piece of advice for the apprentice writer is that whenever he uses a pronoun, he should check to see whether there is a noun in the previous group of words that he could put in the place of the pronoun. Let's apply this advice to the sentence ''Mayor Worthington, acting on the advice of his physician, resigned the office of the president of the council, and the council, responding to a mandate from the voters, was swift to accept it.'' There are three neuter, singular nouns in the previous group of words to which the final pronoun **it** could refer: **advice, office, mandate.** But when we put each of these nouns, successively, in the place of **it,** we see that none of them names what the council accepted. If we pondered the sentence long enough, we might eventually figure out that what the council accepted was the mayor's **resignation.** But since there is no such noun in the previous group of words, the writer could avoid even a momentary vagueness if he would use the noun phrase **his resignation** instead of the pronoun **it.**

Grammar

The use of the pronouns **this** and **that** to refer to a whole idea in a previous clause or sentence has been a common practice for a long time in spoken English, and this use is now becoming common in written English as well. Although the practice is gaining the approval of usage, a writer should be aware that by using the demonstrative pronouns **this** or **that** to refer to a whole idea in the previous clause or sentence he runs the risk that the reference of the pronoun will be vague or ambiguous for his readers. If he doesn't want to run that risk, he can use the **this** or **that** (or their corresponding plurals, **these** and **those**) as a demonstrative adjective modifying some summary noun. Thus, instead of saying, "I enjoyed the mountains, but this revealed to me that I really prefer a vacation at the beach," the writer may decide to protect his meaning by saying, "I enjoyed the mountains, but this experience revealed to me that I really prefer a vacation at the beach."

The use of the relative pronoun **which** to refer to a whole idea in the main clause rather than to a specific noun is also becoming more common and acceptable. But there is a risk in this use similar to the one that attends the use of **this** or **that** to refer to a whole idea. The writer who worries about whether his reader may be even momentarily baffled by the sentence "I decided to break the engagement with my girlfriend, which distressed my parents very much" will supply a summary noun to serve as the antecedent for **which:** "I decided to break the engagement with my girlfriend, a decision which distressed my parents very much."

The writer who has mastered the use of the pronoun has mastered a good part of the craft of writing lucid prose.

25

An introductory verbal or verbal phrase must find its "doer" in the subject of the main clause.

VERBAL PHRASE , SUBJECT | VERB

Examples of "dangling" verbal phrases:

1 Walking on the sidewalk, the Volkswagen ran over me.
2 By returning evil for evil, no permanent good can be accomplished.
3 Refusing to be inducted into the army, the World Boxing Association stripped Muhammad Ali of his title.
4 To accomplish this end, it is necessary for us to study grammar and usage.

In English, an introductory verbal or verbal phrase (participles, gerunds, and infinitives) naturally adheres to the subject of the main clause. When the subject of the main clause is not the "doer" of the action indicated in the verbal, we say that the verbal **dangles**—that it is not attached to the proper agent. By ignoring this basic principle of English grammar, a writer often produces a ludicrous sentence, like the first example above, and in all cases says what he did not intend to say.

To prevent dangling verbals, the writer should make sure that the subject of the main clause is the *doer* of the action specified in the preceding verbal. If the writers of the sample sentences above had observed this caution, they would have revised their sentences to read:

Grammar

1 Walking on the sidewalk, I was run over by a Volkswagen. **OR:** A Volkswagen ran over me while I was walking on the sidewalk.

2 By returning evil for evil, one can accomplish no permanent good.

3 Refusing to be inducted into the army, Muhammad Ali was stripped of his title by the World Boxing Association. **OR:** The World Boxing Association stripped Muhammad Ali of his title for refusing to be inducted into the army.

4 To accomplish this end, we must study grammar and usage.

26
Misplaced modifiers lead to a misreading of the sentence.

Examples of misplaced modifiers:

1 Anyone who reads a newspaper **frequently** will notice that many people are now concerned about pollution.

2 The author seems to be saying that people who refer to the past **constantly** follow the same ritual themselves.

3 He has **only** a face that a mother could love.

4 The teacher distributed examinations to the students **covered with splotches of ink.**

5 **After you entered the park,** the sponsors of the Summerfest decided that you would not have to spend any more money at the concession stands.

6 The plot of the story is a simple one, but there is little chance of the reader's becoming bored **because the author uses many clever devices to advance the plot.**

Because English is a language that depends heavily on word order, related words must often be placed as close as possible to one another. Adverbial and adjectival modifiers especially must be placed as close as possible to words that they modify. Failure to juxtapose related words often leads to a misreading, to a reading different from what the writer intended.

In the first two sample sentences above, we have examples of what are called **squinting modifiers,** modifiers that look in two directions at once. In the first sentence, the adverb **frequently** is sitting between two verbs that grammatically and semantically it could modify—**reads** and **will notice.** If the writer intends the adverb to modify the act of reading rather than the act of noticing, he should shift the position of **frequently** so that the sentence reads as follows: **Anyone who frequently reads a newspaper will notice that many people are now concerned about pollution.** If, however, the writer intends the adverb to modify the act of noticing, he should shift **frequently** to a position between **will** and **notice** or after **notice.**

In the second sample sentence, the adverb **constantly** is likewise sitting between two verbs that it could modify—**refer** and **follow.** Shifting the adverb to a position before the verb **refer** will make the sentence say what the writer probably meant it to say: **The author seems to be saying that people who constantly refer to the past follow the same ritual themselves.**

Because **only** in the third sample sentence is placed in the wrong clause in the sentence, it modifies **a face.** The writer of that sentence could avoid eliciting chuckles from his readers if he would put **only** in the clause where it belongs and make his sentence read as follows: **He has a face that only a mother could love.**

Notice how shifting the position of the modifiers in the fourth, fifth, and sixth sample sentences makes the sentences say what they were intended to say:

Grammar

> The teacher distributed to the students examinations covered with splotches of ink.

> The sponsors of the Summerfest decided that after you entered the park you would not have to spend any more money at the concession stands.

> The plot of the story is a simple one, but because the author uses many clever devices to advance the plot, there is little chance of the reader's becoming bored.

Reading sentences aloud will sometimes reveal the misplacement of modifying words, phrases, and clauses.

27

Preserve parallel structure by using units of the same grammatical kind.

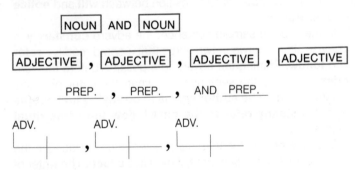

Examples of breakdown in parallelism:

1 The old beliefs about theft have been rejected as **superstitions** and **detrimental** to one's prestige.

   (*noun and adjective*)

2 He was a **miser,** a **bachelor,** and **egotistical.**

   (*noun, noun, adjective*)

3 John was **healthy, wealthy,** and an **athlete.**

(*adjective, adjective, noun*)

4 First of all, Daisy was an **adult, married,** and **had a young daughter.**

(*noun, adjective, verb phrase*)

5 Lincoln was a man **of the people, for the people,** and **loved by the people.**

(*prepositional phrase, prepositional phrase, participial phrase*)

6 The President commended the steelworkers **for their patriotism** and **because they did not ask for a wage increase.**

(*prepositional phrase, adverb clause*)

7 I enjoy reading simply **for personal enlightenment** and **to develop mental sharpness.**

(*prepositional phrase, infinitive phrase*)

8 The admen **not only** convince the reader that the Continental is a luxury car **but also** that the car confers status on its owner.

(*violation of parallelism with correlative conjunctions*)

The principle governing parallel structure is that a pair or a series (three or more) of coordinate units should be of the same kind—nouns with nouns, adjectives with adjectives, not a mixture of nouns and adjectives. A breakdown in parallelism wrenches coherence because it disrupts the expectation that is set up for a reader when a series starts out with one kind of unit and then suddenly shifts to another kind.

The obvious way to correct a breakdown in parallelism is to convert all the members of the pair or the series to units of the same grammatical kind. Sometimes a writer has an either/or choice for the conversion, as in the second sample sentence above: **He was a miser, a bachelor, and egotistical** (noun, noun, adjective). Here the writer has the option of converting all the units of the series into nouns **(He was a miser, a bachelor, and an egotist)** or into adjectives **(He**

was miserly, single, and egotistical). Likewise, the writer of the sixth sample sentence above can convert both units of the pair into prepositional phrases (**for their patriotism** and **for their restraint** in not asking for a wage increase) or into adverb clauses **(because they were patriotic** and **because they did not ask for a wage increase).**

In the third sample sentence above, however, the writer does not have an either/or choice. He can convert the three predicate complements into adjectives (He was **healthy, wealthy,** and **athletic**), but since there is no noun equivalent of the adjective **healthy** (**a valetudinarian** is not quite right) nor a single-word noun equivalent of the adjective **wealthy** (he would have to use **a rich man**), he cannot convert all the complements into nouns.

It should be pointed out that although grammatical options are frequently available, one of the options will usually be stylistically preferable to the other. The writer has to exercise his judgment in making the better stylistic choice.

The breakdown in parallelism in the eighth sample sentence above is of a slightly different kind. This sample sentence illustrates a violation of parallelism when correlative conjunctions are used: **either . . . or; neither . . . nor; not (only) . . . but (also).** The principle operating with correlative conjunctions is that **the same grammatical structure must be on the right-hand side of both conjunctions.** We can more easily see the breakdown in parallelism if we lay out the eighth sample sentence in two layers:

The admen **not only** convince the reader that the Continental is
a luxury car

but also that the car confers status on its owner.

On the right-hand side of **not only** the writer has this grammatical sequence: a verb **(convince),** a noun **(the reader),**

and a noun clause **(that the Continental is a luxury car).**
On the right-hand side of **but also,** however, he has only the
noun clause **(that the car confers status on its owner).** He
can fix up the parallelism in either of two ways:

> The admen **not only** convince the reader that the Continental is
> a luxury car
>
> > **but also** convince the reader that the car confers
> > status on its owner.
>
> > **OR** (probably preferable stylistically):
>
> The admen convince the reader **not only** that the Continental is
> a luxury car
>
> > **but also** that the car confers
> > status on its owner.

In both revisions we now have the same grammatical structures on the right-hand side of both correlative conjunctions.

Note how parallelism is preserved in the following two
sentences using correlative conjunctions:

> **Either** he will love the one and hate the other, **or** he will hate the
> one and love the other.
>
> He will **either** love the one and hate the other **or** hate the one
> and love the other.

The principle governing parallelism: **like must be yoked
with like.**

Grammar

28

Use the subordinate conjunction that if it will prevent a possible misreading.

Examples where it would be advisable to insert **that**:

1 My father believed‸his doctor, who was a boyhood friend, was wholly trustworthy.

2 A more realistic person would probably assert‸these statements about the ad were frivolous and sentimental.

3 He discovered‸the radio and the tape recorder in his roommate's closet had been stolen.

4 The author reported‸as soon as a Jew became intensely depressed in camp and lost all purpose for living, death came shortly after.

5 Professor Clements maintained‸Communism rejected capitalism and democracy rejected collective ownership.

The tendency of any language is toward economy of means. So we elide syllables in such contractions as **he's, she'll, we'd, won't,** and we resort to such common elliptical expressions as **not all (of) the men; he is taller than I (am tall); when (I was) in the fourth grade, I went to the zoo with my father.** We also frequently omit the conjunction **that** which introduces a noun clause serving as the object of a verb, as in "He said he was going" and "He announced I was a candidate for office."

Whether to use the conjunction **that** in written prose will be a problem only when a noun clause is being used as the direct object of a verb—but not in every instance of such use. If there is no chance that the syntax of a sentence will be misread, it is all right, even in written prose, to omit **that.** But if there is a chance that a noun phrase following the verb may be read as the object of the verb rather than as the subject of the subsequent clause, then the writer should prevent even a momentary misreading by inserting **that** at the head of the noun clause. What follows may make all of this clearer.

In a sentence like **He said he was going,** it is safe to omit **that** after **said** because **he,** being a pronoun in the nominative case (see GLOSSARY), cannot possibly be read as the object of **said.** But in a sentence like the first sample sentence above, it is not only possible but likely that the noun phrase **his doctor** will momentarily be read as the object of **believed (he believed his doctor).** Of course, as soon as the reader comes on the predicate **was wholly trustworthy,** he realizes that he has misread the sentence, and he has to back up and reread the sentence as the writer intended it to be read. But the writer could have prevented that initial misreading by inserting **that** after **believed—My father believed that his doctor, who was a boyhood friend, was wholly trustworthy.** Then the sentence can be read in only one way—the way in which the writer intended it to be read.

Note how the insertion of **that** where the caret $(\wedge)$ is in the other sample sentences prevents an initial misreading of the sentences. Whenever a reader has to reread a sentence in order to make sense of it, the writer is usually the one to blame. Inserting **that** where it is necessary or advisable will save the reader from having to reread a sentence.

29

Avoid the careless or indefensible use of sentence fragments.

Examples of questionable sentence fragments:

1 **The reason for this reaction being that people are flattered by courtesy.**

Grammar

2 I shall not try to defend myself on the grounds that I did not violate the regulation. **Although I could offer the excuse that I didn't know that such a regulation existed.**

3 Both men are alike in that they try to help people only if the effort does not result in too much trouble for themselves. **Herenger, in his idea that it is good to help someone with "so little trouble to himself," and the Baron, who believes in giving money to someone as long as there is no further responsibility involved.**

4 The bond between Gretta and Michael was strong enough to make him face death rather than be separated from her. **The tragedy here that such a love could not be consummated and that one so young should be cut off just at the dawn of life.**

5 Much information about a topic can be brought forth by poetry. **The topic of science, in particular, because science is basically factual.**

A sentence fragment can be defined as a string of words, between an initial capital letter and a period or question mark, that lacks a subject or a finite-verb predicate (or both) or that has a subject and a finite-verb predicate but is made part of a larger structure by a relative pronoun **(who, which, that)** or by a subordinating conjunction (**because, if, when,** etc.).

The string of words in the first example above is a sentence fragment because the subject **reason** lacks a finite-verb predicate. Changing the participle **being** to the finite verb **is** would make that string of words a complete sentence.

The boldface string of words in the second example is a sentence fragment because the subordinating conjunction **although** makes the clause that follows it a part of, or dependent on, a larger structure. The adverb clause introduced by **although** "depends on" the independent clause in the previous sentence, and therefore the adverb clause cannot stand by itself. This example may be more the result of carelessness in punctuating the sentence than the result of ignorance of what constitutes a complete sentence, for the sentence fragment here can be eliminated simply by changing the period after **regulation** to a comma and reducing the first letter in **Although** to lowercase **(I shall not try to defend myself on the grounds that I did not violate the regulation, although I could offer the excuse that I didn't know that such a regulation existed).**

The boldface string of words in the third example is a sentence fragment because it lacks an independent clause. It lacks an independent clause because neither **Herenger** nor **Baron,** which appear to be "subjects," has a predicate verb. Likewise, **The tragedy** in the fourth example and **The topic of science** in the fifth lack predicate verbs.

Whether a string of words constitutes a complete sentence or only a sentence fragment is a grammatical concern; whether the use of a sentence fragment is appropriate in a particular context and is therefore justifiable is a rhetorical or stylistic concern. It is a fact of life that sometimes we communicate with one another in sentence fragments. Take for instance the following exchange:

Where are you going tonight?
The movies.
With whom?
Jack.
Where?
The Palace.
What time?
About 8:30.
By car?
No, by bus.
Can I go along?
Sure.

Grammar

Once the context of that dialogue was established, both speakers communicated with one another in fragments. Notice, though, that the dialogue had to be initiated by a complete sentence (the question **Where are you going tonight?**) and that later the first speaker had to resort again to a complete sentence **(Can I go along?)** because there was no way to phrase that question clearly in a fragmentary way.

Native speakers of a language can converse in fragments because each of them is capable of mentally supplying what is missing from an utterance. When in response to the initial question the second speaker answers, ''The movies,'' that phrase conveys a meaning because the first speaker is able to supply, mentally and perhaps subconsciously, the missing elements in the fragmentary reply: **(I am going to) the movies.**

All of us have encountered sentence fragments in the written prose of some very reputable writers. Predicateless sentences are most likely to be found in mood-setting descriptive and narrative prose, as in this first paragraph of Charles Dickens's novel *Bleak House:*

> London. Michaelmas Term lately over, and the Lord Chancellor sitting in Lincoln's Inn Hall. Implacable November weather. As much mud in the streets, as if the waters had but newly retired from the face of the earth, and it would not be wonderful to meet a Megalosaurus, forty feet long or so, waddling like an elephantine lizard up Holborn Hill. Smoke lowering down from chimney-pots, making a soft black drizzle, with flakes of soot in it as big as full-grown snow-flakes—gone into mourning, one might imagine, for the death of the sun. Dogs, undistinguishable in mire. Horses, scarcely better; splashed to their blinkers. Foot passengers, jostling one another's umbrellas, in a general infection of illtemper, and losing their foothold at street-corners, where tens of thousands of other foot passengers have been slipping and sliding since the day broke (if

this day ever broke), adding new deposits to the crust upon crust of mud, sticking at those points tenaciously to the pavement and accumulating at compound interest.

In that paragraph, there are a few clauses (that is, groups of words with a subject and a finite-verb predicate), but the paragraph is composed predominantly of nouns and noun phrases, some of them modified by participial phrases. But although the passage is largely lacking in predications made by finite verbs, the sequence of sentence fragments creates effects that Dickens could not have achieved—or could not have achieved as well—with complete sentences.

The point of citing these examples of spoken and written discourse is that sentence fragments are a part of the English language (in that sense they are "grammatical"), that in certain contexts they do communicate meaning, and that in some circumstances and for some purposes they are appropriate and therefore acceptable, effective, and even stylistically desirable. But the writer should be aware of what he is doing. He should know that he is writing a sentence fragment rather than a complete sentence; otherwise he will be guilty of a *careless* use of a sentence fragment. And he should have some purpose or effect in mind when he uses a sentence fragment; otherwise he will be guilty of an *indefensible* use of a sentence fragment.

30

Independent clauses cannot be spliced together simply with a comma.

Grammar

Examples of comma splices:

1 We are not allowed to think for ourselves, that privilege is reserved for administrators.
2 Last summer my family saw the whole United States from the inside of an air-conditioned trailer, outside the weather ranged from cool to hot, from dry to muggy.
3 Our minds are never challenged by the television set, it is just so much easier to sit there than to read a book.
4 You will have to choose your vocation yourself, however, you should consider what others have told you about the hazards of various jobs.

A comma splice is the joining of independent clauses with a comma. It occurs only in compound sentences—that is, in sentences composed of two or more independent clauses. A comma splice is an error in punctuation, but since punctuation is, for the written language, the equivalent of vocal intonation in the spoken language, this error in punctuation can also be considered an error in grammar.

Independent clauses must be joined either by a coordinating conjunction **(and, but, or, for, nor, yet, so)** or by a semicolon. In addition to these two ways of properly splicing independent clauses, there are two other ways of fixing up the comma splice: by making separate sentences of the two clauses and by subordinating one of the clauses. Using each of these methods in turn, let us correct the comma splice in the first sample sentence above.

(a) Insert the appropriate coordinating conjunction after the comma:

We are not allowed to think for ourselves, **for** that privilege is reserved for administrators.

(b) Substitute a semicolon for the comma:

We are not allowed to think for ourselves **;** that privilege is reserved for administrators.

(c) Subordinate one of the independent clauses:

We are not allowed to think for ourselves, **because** that privilege is reserved for administrators.

(d) Put a period at the end of the first independent clause and begin a new sentence with the first word of the second independent clause:

We are not allowed to think for ourselves **.** **T**hat privilege is reserved for administrators.

Although these four ways of fixing up a comma splice are always available, one of these options will usually be better in a particular instance. In the case of the first sample sentence, splicing the two clauses together with a semicolon would probably be best: **We are not allowed to think for ourselves; that privilege is reserved for administrators.** The semicolon here effects the closest union of the two related clauses and best points up the irony between the thoughts in the two clauses. We have made our choice of the semicolon on stylistic grounds; grammatically, the other three options are equally correct.

See **66** and **67** in the punctuation section for the proper use of the semicolon.

Grammar

31

**Do not run independent clauses together without a
conjunction or the proper punctuation.**

Examples of independent clauses run together:

1 Why am I qualified to speak on this subject I just finished three
dreadful years of high school.
2 Those shiny red apples sitting on my desk pleased me very
much they were tokens of affection from my students.
3 Two suspects were arrested last week one of them was a
cripple.
4 Leggatt was blackballed for having killed a man thus he would
never be able to work on a ship again.

The term commonly used to label two or more independent
clauses that have been run together without any conjunction
or punctuation is **fused sentence** or **run-on sentence.**
Fused sentences are not as common in writing as comma
splices, but when they do occur, they are even more of a
stumbling block for a reader than comma splices are. If the
writers of the sample sentences above had read their string of
words aloud, they would have detected a natural stopping
place—a place where the expression of one thought ended
and the expression of another thought began.

Fused sentences can be corrected in the same four ways
that comma splices can be corrected:

(a) Join the independent clauses with the appropriate
coordinating conjunction:

Those shiny red apples sitting on my desk pleased me very much, **for** they were tokens of affection from my students.

(b) Splice the independent clauses with a semicolon:

Two suspects were arrested last week; one of them was a cripple.

(c) Subordinate one of the independent clauses:

Because Leggatt was blackballed for having killed a man, he would never be able to work on a ship again.

(d) Make separate sentences of the independent clauses:

Why am I qualified to speak on this subject? I just finished three dreadful years of high school.

As in the case of comma splices, all four of these ways are usually available for correcting a fused sentence, but in a particular instance, one of them will usually be better than the others. Some of the sample sentences do not readily lend themselves to correction by all four means. For instance, because the first sample sentence fuses a question and a statement—**Why am I qualified to speak on this subject** (question) and **I just finished three dreadful years of high school** (statement)—it lends itself to correction only by the fourth method, that of making separate sentences of the two clauses.

Reading one's prose aloud will usually disclose instances where independent clauses have been run together.

Grammar

32

Choose words and put them together so that they make sense.

Examples of confused or puzzling sentences:

1 This same technique of philosophical truths expressed tersely and lyrically, which we often see in Johnson's works, is very prevalent in *Rasselas*.

2 Much later in the story, the dinner conversation the function of the "small talk" seems to be about the old times.

3 The youth, rejected by his parents, by the world, by God, and tragically and ultimately he has rejected himself.

4 William Faulkner presents in his short story "Barn Burning" a human character that is as nonhuman as is feasible to a person's mind.

5 Now in the third stanza, the poet starts his descent. He brings about his conclusion of the boy, which can be paralleled to mankind.

6 Of course, this situation of rundown houses is not always the case, but instead the high rent that the tenants have to pay, which leaves little money for anything else.

A confused or puzzling sentence is one that because of some flaw in the choice or disposition of words reveals no meaning or only a vague meaning. We could say of such a sentence that it is a "non-English" sentence—a sentence that is semantically or grammatically impossible in the English language. A sentence like "The ice cube froze" is a non-English sentence because the meanings of **ice cube** and **froze** are incompatible. We can say, "The water froze," but we are uttering "nonsense" if we say, "The ice cube froze." The phrase **his conclusion of the boy** in the fifth sample sentence above is an instance of a choice of incompatible words. A sentence like "Harshly me teacher scolded the yesterday" is a non-English sentence because English grammar does not allow that order of words. To make sense, those words have to be disposed in an order like this: **The teacher scolded me harshly yesterday.** Each of the first, second, third, and sixth sample sentences has some flaw in syntax that prevents the writer's meaning from getting through to the reader.

If the reader cannot figure out what the writer meant to say, he often cannot even analyze what went wrong with the sentence, and he certainly cannot suggest to the writer how the bewildering sentence might be fixed up. He can only point out to the writer that the sentence makes no sense and urge him to try again to say what he meant to say.

What were the writers of the sample sentences trying to say?

Style

Style is the result of the choices that a writer makes from the available vocabulary and syntactical resources of a language. A writer may not choose—or should not choose

☐ **Words and structures that are not part of the language:**

The defendants have **klinded** the case to the Supreme Court.

(*no such word in the English language*)

All gas stations **have being closed** for the duration of the emergency.

(*no such verb structure in the English language*)

☐ **Words and structures that make no sense:**

The mountains lucidly transgressed sentient rocks.

(*a grammatical but nonsensical sentence*)

☐ **Words and structures that do not convey a clear, unambiguous meaning:**

The teacher gave the papers to the students that were chosen by the committee.

(*was it the **papers** or the **students** that were chosen by the committee?*)

Aside from these unavailable or inadvisable choices, however, the rich vocabulary and the flexible syntax of the English language offer the writer a number of alternative but synonymous ways of saying something. One may choose to use an active verb or a passive verb:

He reported the accident to the police.

OR: The accident was reported by him to the police.

or one may shift the position of some modifiers:

He reported the accident to the police when he was ready.

OR: When he was ready, he reported the accident to the police.

or one may substitute synonymous words and phrases:

He informed the police about the accident at the intersection.

OR: John notified Sergeant James Murphy about the collision at the corner of Fifth and Main.

A number of other stylistic choices may be open to the writer. For instance, he may have to decide whether to write a long sentence or to break up the sentence into a series of separate short sentences; whether to write a compound sentence or to subordinate one of the clauses; whether to modify a noun with an adjective clause or with a participial phrase or with merely an adjective: whether to use literal language or figurative language; whether to use a ''big'' word or a simple word (*altercation* or *quarrel*), a specific word or a general word (*sauntered* or *walked*), a formal word or a colloquial word (*children* or *kids*).

Grammar will determine whether a stylistic choice is *correct*—that is, whether a particular locution is allowable by the conventions of the language. Rhetoric will determine whether

Style

a stylistic choice is *effective*—that is, whether a particular locution conveys the intended meaning with the clarity, economy, emphasis, and tone appropriate to the subject matter, occasion, audience, and desired effect.

This section on style asks the writer to consider whether he has made the best choice of words and arrangement of words. Questions about style are not so much questions about *right* and *wrong* as questions about *good, better, best.*

40

Choose the right word for what you intend to say.

Examples of wrong words:

1 The typical surfer has long **ignominious** hair bleached by the **torpid** sun.
2 By the time we reached Phoenix, we had spent our food allotment and were faced with the gloomy **aspect** of starving to death.
3 If you do not **here** from me within three weeks, give me a call.
4 The shortstop played very **erotically** in the first game of the doubleheader.

A word is labeled "wrong" when its meaning does not fit the context, does not express the intended meaning. The most obvious instance of a "wrong word" is the substitution, usually due to carelessness, of a homonym (a like-sounding word) for the intended word, like **here** for **hear** (see the third example above), **through** for **threw, there** for **their, sole** for **soul.**

Another kind of "wrong word" is what is called a **malapropism,** after Mrs. Malaprop in Sheridan's play *The Rivals.*

40 Wrong Word and Faulty Predication

Mrs. Malaprop would say things like "as headstrong as an *allegory* on the banks of the Nile." There is a malapropism in the fourth example above. The writer has heard the expression "he played erratically," but by using the approximate-sounding word **erotically,** he has produced a "howler." **Aspect** in the second example above makes some sense, but *prospect* would come closer to expressing what the writer probably had in mind.

The most common kind of "wrong word" is usually the result of a writer's using a word that is new and somewhat unfamiliar to him. In the first example above, the denotative meaning of **ignominious** is "disgraceful, shameful," but although we can speak of "an ignominious act," the word is inappropriate when attached to **hair.** In the same sentence, if the writer meant to say that the sun was sluggish, **torpid** is the right word; but "torrid sun" comes closer to what he probably meant to say.

Another common instance of "wrong word" can be designated by the term **faulty predication.** A faulty predication occurs when the predicate of a clause (either the verb itself or the whole verb phrase) does not fit semantically or syntactically with the subject of a clause. In other words, the predicate of a clause must fit *grammatically* with the subject (e.g. see sample sentences 8, 9, and 10 below) and must be compatible *in meaning* with the subject (e.g. see sample sentence 1 below). Here are some examples of incompatible predicates:

1 A thief and a liar **are vices** that we should avoid.
2 His purpose **was a ridicule and exposure** of the business mentality.
3 The first section of the poem **is** nothing more than Dryden's reasons for liking Mr. Oldham.

Style

4 He cited an article that **was a dual authorship.**

5 Edgar Lee Masters is saying that the shootings and the hangings are indefensible and that justice **seems** only for the rich.

6 Abused children **should not be tolerated** in our society.

7 The source of Hemingway's title **is taken** from a sermon by John Donne.

8 The reason why she did not come to class **is because she was sick.**

9 The beach **is where I get my worst sunburn.**

10 An example of honesty **is when someone finds a wallet and brings it to the police.**

Faulty predications often occur when some form of the verb **to be** serves as the predicate verb, as in the first four examples and in the last three. Because the verb **to be** is setting up an equation between the subject and the complement, the complement part of the sentence must fit semantically and syntactically with the subject part of the sentence. In the first example, for instance, the complement **vices** does not fit semantically with the subject **a thief and a liar** (thieves and liars are not vices). The adverb clauses following the verb **to be** in the eighth, ninth, and tenth examples do not fit syntactically, because adverb clauses cannot serve as complements for the verb **to be** (no more than a simple adverb could serve as the complement for the verb **to be:** ''he is swiftly''). The fifth, sixth, and seventh examples above are instances of faulty predication with verbs other than the verb **to be.**

Revisions of the faulty predications:

1 A thief and a liar exemplify (or practice) vices that we should avoid. (Or: Thievery and lying are vices that we should avoid.)

2 His purpose was to ridicule and expose the business mentality.

3 The first section of the poem presents nothing more than Dryden's reasons for liking Mr. Oldham.

46

40 Wrong Word and Faulty Predication

4 He cited an article that had a dual authorship. (Or: He cited an article that was written by two authors.)

5 Edgar Lee Masters is saying that the shootings and the hangings are indefensible and that justice seems to be reserved only for the rich.

6 Abused children should be removed from their parents. (Or: The abuse of children should not be tolerated in our society.)

7 The source of Hemingway's title is a sermon by John Donne.

8 The reason why she did not come to class is that she was sick.

9 The beach is the place where I get my worst sunburn.

10 Honesty is exemplified when someone finds a wallet and brings it to the police.

But now we must point out an important exception to the principle of semantic compatibility between the subject and the predicate. Whenever a metaphor is used, there is, in a sense, a semantic incompatibility between the subject and the predicate. On the literal level, it is nonsense to say "That man is a lion in battle," because, strictly speaking, we cannot predicate lionhood of a human being. But we soon develop enough sophistication in language to recognize that in instances like this the predicate term is being used in a transferred or figurative sense. We understand that the man is not being literally equated with a lion—that is, the man is not really a lion—but that he is being compared to a lion—that is, the man has certain ferocious qualities that remind us of a ravaging lion. Recognizing the metaphorical use of the word *lion,* we do not feel that this complement is semantically incompatible with the subject.

Until a writer gains the assured familiarity with words that will prevent the choice of the wrong word for what he intends to say, he will have to be unusually cautious in his choice of words, and he may have to consult a dictionary frequently.

41

Choose the precise word for what you want to say.

Examples of imprecise words:

1 I liked the movie *Love Story* because it was **beautiful.**
2 What most impressed me about the poem was the poet's **descriptive** language.
3 Has-been athletes always have a **sore** look on their face.
4 To prevent her from catching a cold, he insisted that she wear the **gigantic** galoshes.
5 Honesty is a **thing** that we should value highly.
6 Jane sold her car, **as** she was planning to take a trip to Europe.

Whereas a "wrong word" misses the target entirely, an "imprecise word" hits all around the bull's-eye but never on dead center.

The word **beautiful** in the first example above is too general to convey a precise meaning. A reader's response to a general word like that would be to ask, "In what way was the movie beautiful?" If the writer had said "poignant" or "believable" or "edifying" or "inspiring" or "visually pleasing," the reader might want some more particulars, but at least he would have a clearer idea of why the writer liked the movie.

The word **descriptive** in the second example is too vague. Expressions like "the poet's vivid, sensory diction" or "the poet's simple, concrete words" or "the poet's specific adjectives for indicating colors" would give the reader a more exact idea of the kind of descriptive language that impressed the writer of the sentence.

Sore in the third example is ambiguous—that is, it has more than one meaning in the context. If the writer wants to convey the notion that the former athletes were disgruntled, let him say that "they have an angry look on their face" or simply that "they look angry," but if he wants to convey the notion that the former athletes exhibited physical discomfort, let him say that "they have a painful look on their face"—or in some other way say that their faces reflect their aching wounds.

Gigantic in the fourth example is hyperbolic, or exaggerated. Unless the writer of that sentence deliberately used the hyperbolic **gigantic** for humorous effect, he should use a more proportionate word like *big* or *heavy* or *ungainly*.

In the spoken medium, we often do not have the leisure to search for the precise word; we utter the first word that offers itself. In response to the question "How did you like him?" we might say, "Oh, I thought he was nice enough." If the person with whom we are speaking is not satisfied by our general word of approval, *nice,* he can ask us to be more specific. In the written medium, however, the situation is quite different: we do have the leisure to search for a precise word, and we are not available to the reader who may want more specific information. While we may be able to get by in the oral medium with a catchall word like **thing,** as in the fifth sample above, we should strive for more precision in the written medium and say something like **Honesty is a *virtue* that we should value highly.** Consulting a thesaurus or, better yet, a dictionary that discriminates the meanings of synonyms will frequently yield the exact word for our intended meaning.

The subordinating conjunction **as** carries a variety of meanings, and it is not always possible to tell from the context which of its many meanings it carries in a particular sentence. In the sixth sample sentence above **(Jane sold her car, *as* she was planning to take a trip to Europe),** we cannot tell whether **as** is being used in its sense of "because'' or ''since'' or in its sense of ''when'' or ''while.'' So we should use the conjunction that exactly expresses our intended meaning: **because** she was planning; **when** she was planning; **while** she was planning. We should reserve the conjunction **as** for those contexts in which there is no possibility of ambiguity, as in sentences like ''In that situation, he voted exactly **as** he should'' and ''Do **as** I say.''

42

Choose words that are appropriate to the context.

Examples of inappropriate words:

1 Before the unbelieving **orbs** of the other players, he advances his piece on the board, arresting his **manual appendage** only when he sees that he is going to land on Boardwalk.

2 With **mendacious sangfroid,** he remarked, ''You don't have to apologize. I've known lots of people who have done it,'' and in the same **prevaricating** tone, he **asseverates,** ''Virtue is as virtue does.''

3 The conclusion that I have come to is that **kids** should not have to suffer for the sins of their fathers.

4 My senator tries to act **real groovy and all,** but despite all the **mod rags** he affects, he still gives out with all that graybeard **jive** about the importance of getting a good education so that you can get a good job so that you can afford to maintain a prestigious **pad** and **wheels.**

A word is inappropriate to its context if it does not fit, if it is out of tune with, the subject matter, the occasion, the audience, or the personality of the speaker or writer. It is conspicuous by its inharmonious presence.

No word in isolation can be labeled ''inappropriate''; it

must be seen in the company of other words before it can be declared "inappropriate." Although one would feel safer in making a judgment if one had a larger context, the boldfaced words in the first two examples above seem to be inappropriate because they are too elegant or inflated for the subject matter—a game of Monopoly in the first sentence, a reporting of a remark made at a cocktail party in the second sentence. There seems to be no good reason for the writer of the first sentence not to use the simpler, less pretentious *eyes* for **orbs** and *hand* for **manual appendage.** Young writers consciously striving to enlarge their vocabulary often produce sentences like the second example. Instead of using a thesaurus to find an accurate or precise word for what they want to say, they use it to find an unusual or a polysyllabic word that will make their prose sound "literary." The one hopeful thing that can be said about such writers is that if they are ambitious enough to want to expand their working vocabulary, they will very soon develop enough sophistication about language to know when it is appropriate, and when it is inappropriate, to use "big words."

The more common fault of inappropriateness, however, is diction that is too colloquial, too slangy, for its formal context. Although there are contexts where the colloquial **kids** would be more appropriate than the word *children,* the third example above seems not to be one of those contexts. There are contexts where slang and even the jargon of particular social groups will be perfectly appropriate, but the slang in the fourth sample sentence above seems to be out of tune with the subject matter and with the majority of the other words in the sentence. Even if the writer of that sentence could justify the use of such terms as **groovy, mod rags,** and **jive** as being appropriate to his personality, he could not justify the use of **pad** and **wheels** in that part of the sentence where apparently he is paraphrasing the pious platitudes of his senator. Even if the senator had been addressing a group of hippies, he would not have used **pad** for *home* or **wheels** for *automobile*.

Since dictionaries, thesauruses, and handbooks will not be of much help in telling a writer when a word is appropriate, the writer will have to rely on the criteria of subject matter, occasion, audience, desired effect, and personality of the author. Another way to put the precept is to say that the writer's "voice" must remain consistent with the overall tone he has established in a particular piece of writing.

43
Use the proper idiom.

Examples of lapse of idiom:

1 Although I agree **to** a few of Socrates' principles, I must disagree **to** many of them.
2 Conformity has been a common tendency throughout **the** American history.
3 Blake then **differs** the two introductory pieces by contrasting the simplicity and innocence of the child with the maturity and sophistication of the adult.
4 Harold and the star quarterback from Steuben High also **compared** in being able to throw a clothesline pass.
5 It's these special characters and their motives that I intend **on concentrating** in this paper.
6 Abner had no interest or respect **for** the boy.

To label a locution "unidiomatic" is to indicate that native speakers of the language do not say it that way—in any dialect of the language. Unidiomatic expressions are one of the commonest weaknesses to be found in the prose of unpracticed writers. Why do lapses of idiom occur so frequently? They occur often because many writers have not paid close enough attention—have not attuned their ears—to the way native speakers of the language, including themselves, say something. In trying to express themselves on paper, they put down expressions that they would never use in the spoken medium and that they have never heard any other native speaker use.

No native speaker of the English language, for instance, would use the article **the** in the phrase **throughout the American history** (see the second example above). However, an American speaker would say "He was in the hospital," whereas a British speaker would say "He was in hospital." Some Asian speakers have trouble with the English article, because their language does not use a part of speech like our article.

Lapses of idiom frequently occur with prepositions. A number of prepositions fit idiomatically with the verb **agree,** but the writer must attune his ear to the proper idiom in the proper place. He can say **agree to** in an expression like "He agreed to the conditions we laid down." He can say **agree on** in an expression like "They can't agree on the wording of the proposal." The preposition that fits idiomatically with the sense of **agree** and **disagree** in the first example above is **with:** "I agree **with** a few of Socrates' principles" and "I disagree **with** many of them."

Unidiomatic prepositions often appear in compounded phrases, as in the sixth example above. The preposition **for** does fit with **respect** ("respect for the boy"), but it does not fit with **interest** ("interest for the boy"). In such cases, the idiomatic preposition must be inserted for both members of the compound, e.g. "Abner had no interest **in,** or respect **for,** the boy."

In phrasing the third, fourth, and fifth sentences above, native speakers would say "Blake then **differentiates between** the two introductory pieces . . ." and "Harold and the star quarterback from Steuben High were also **comparable** in their ability to throw . . ." and ". . . that I intend to **concentrate on** in this paper."

What prevents a handbook from setting reliable guidelines for proper idioms is the fact that logic plays little or no part in establishing idiom. If logic played such a part, we would say "He looked *down* the word in the dictionary" instead of "He looked *up* the word in the dictionary." Although the eye normally runs down the columns of a dictionary when searching for a word, native speakers say "look up" a word simply because that is the way people have always phrased that locution. An editor or an instructor can call your attention to an unidiomatic expression and insert the correct idiom, but he cannot give you any rule that will prevent other lapses of idiom. You simply have to learn proper idioms by reading more and by listening more intently.

44

Avoid trite expressions.

Examples of trite expressions:

1 I returned from the picnic **tired but happy,** and that night I **slept like a log.**
2 My primary objective in coming to college was to get a **well-rounded education.**
3 The construction of two new hotels was a **giant step forward** for the community.

4 In the last few years, the popularity of ice hockey has grown **by leaps and bounds.**

5 Convinced now that drugs are a temptation for young people, the community must **nip the problem in the bud** before it **runs rampant.**

There is nothing grammatically or idiomatically wrong with a trite expression. A trite expression is *stylistically* objectionable—mainly because it is a *tired* expression. Whether or not an expression is "tired" is, of course, a relative matter. What is a cliché for some readers may be bright-penny new for others. But it would be surprising if the expressions in the examples above were not jaded for most readers.

Trite expressions are combinations of words that have been used so often that they have lost their freshness and even their meaning for most readers. Metaphors are especially prone to staleness. Metaphors like "nip in the bud," "slept like a log," "giant step" were once fresh and cogent; they are now wilted.

Overworked combinations like "a well-rounded education" should be banished from the language, partly because they are boring and partly because they no longer convey a precise meaning. Someone should be daring enough to mint the expression "a well-squared education" and see whether it gains currency.

Be wary of weary words.

45

Rephrase awkwardly constructed sentences.

Examples of awkward sentences:

1 You could get a dose of the best exercise a person could

undertake, walking. I believe a person should walk at a leisurely pace, with no set goal on distance.

2 The football player has had many broken noses, with which he ends up looking like a prizefighter.

3 I and probably everybody else who started drinking beer in their sophomore year of high school thought the only thing to do was get drunk and go to school activities where we could meet and have a good time.

Awkward sentences are sentences so ineptly put together that the resultant jumble of words is difficult to read or understand. An awkward sentence is often the result of a writer's saying something in a wordy, roundabout way rather than in a terse, direct way. The problem is that the one who writes an awkwardly constructed sentence is usually not aware that he has done so; he has to be told that his sentence is awkward.

The ear, however, is a reliable resource for detecting awkward sentences. If a writer adopts the practice of reading his sentences aloud, he will often detect clumsy, odd-sounding combinations of words. Alerted by his ear, he should look for the usual causes of awkwardness: excessive verbiage, words and phrases out of their normal order, successions of prepositional phrases ("the president of the largest chapter of the national fraternity of students of dentistry"), pretentious circumlocutions ("the penultimate month of the year" for "November"), split constructions ("I, chastened by my past experiences, resolved to never consciously and maliciously circulate, even if true, damaging reports about my friends"), successions of rhyming words ("He tries wisely to revise the evidence supplied by his eyes"). In his effort to rephrase the sentence, the writer should try expressing the same thought in the way he would if he were *speaking* the sentence to someone.

The sample sentences above are awkward for a variety of

reasons, but what they all have in common is excessive verbiage. Pruning some of the deadwood, rearranging some of the parts, using simpler, more idiomatic phrases, we can improve the articulation of those clumsy sentences:

1 Walking is the best exercise. A person should walk at a leisurely pace and only as far as he feels like going.
2 The football player has broken his nose so often that he looks like a prizefighter.
3 Like everybody else who started drinking beer in his sophomore year of high school, I thought that getting drunk was the best way to have a good time at school activities.

46

Cut out unnecessary words.

Examples of wordy sentences:

1 He was justified in trying to straighten out his mother on her backward ideas about her attitude toward Negroes. (19 words)
2 In this modern world of today, we must get an education that will prepare us for a job in our vocation in life. (23 words)
3 In the "Garden of Love," the poem relates the sad experience of a child being born into a cruel world. (20 words)
4 The meaning, at least in my own eyes, that he is trying to convey in the poem "Arms and the Boy" is of the evilness of war in that it forces innocent people to take up the instruments of death and destruction and then tries to teach them to love to use them to kill other human beings. (58 words)
5 These rivers do not contain fish, due to the fact that the flow of water is too rapid. (18 words)

A "wordy sentence" is one in which a writer has used more words than are needed to say what he wanted to say. A writer

Style

would soon learn to cultivate restraint if he were charged for every word used, as he is when he sends a telegram. He should not, of course, strive for a "telegraphic" style or a "headline" style, but he should value words so much that he spends them sparingly.

Let us see if we can trim the sample sentences without substantially altering their meaning:

1 He was justified in trying to straighten out his mother's attitude toward Negroes. (13 words)
2 In the modern world, we must get an education that will prepare us for a job. (16 words)
3 The "Garden of Love" relates the sad experience of a child being born into a cruel world. (17 words)
4 As I see it, the poet's thesis in "Arms and the Boy" is that war is evil because it not only forces people to take up arms but makes them use these weapons to kill other human beings. (38 words)
5 These rivers do not contain fish, because they flow too rapidly. (11 words)

Notice that each of the revised sentences uses fewer words than the original. The retrenchment ranges from three words to twenty words. If the writers were being charged a quarter a word, they could probably find other superfluous words to prune. The writer of the fourth sentence, for instance, would probably lop off **As I see it** and **in 'Arms and the Boy,'** and he would condense **to kill other human beings** to **to kill others.**

One should not become obsessed with saving words, but one should seize every opportunity of clearing out obvious deadwood. As Alexander Pope said,

Words are like leaves, and where they most abound,
Much fruit of sense beneath is rarely found.

47

Avoid careless repetition of words and ideas.

Examples of careless repetition:

1 Mr. Bucks, a **fellow colleague,** offered to intercede with the dean.

2 He does not rely on the **surrounding environment** as much as his brother does.

3 The objective point of view accentuates the emotional intensity of the love affair and the **impending** failure that will **eventually happen.**

4 **In Larry's mind** he thinks, "I have never met anyone so absorbed in himself."

5 There are some striking similarities between Segal and Hemingway, for **both** have studied life and love and found them **both** to be failures.

6 After **setting** up camp, we **set** off to watch the sun **set.**

A "careless repetition" refers to the needless repetition of a word in the same sentence (or in adjoining sentences) or to the juxtaposition of synonymous words that produces what is called a **redundancy** or a **tautology.**

The repetition of the pronoun **both** in the fifth example above is especially careless because the repeated pronouns have different antecedents (the first one refers to **Segal** and **Hemingway,** the second to **life** and **love**). The emphasis in this caution about the repetition of a word should be put on the word *needless*. In the sixth sentence above, we have an instance of the same basic verb form **(set)** used in three different senses. Unless the writer here was deliberately playing on words, he would do well to avoid the awkward repetition, saying something like **After preparing camp, we**

went off to watch the sun set. Sometimes it is better to repeat a word, even in the same sentence, than to run the risk of ambiguity or misunderstanding. In a sentence like "She told her mother that her hairdryer was broken," if the ambiguity of the second **her** could not be remedied in some other way, it would be better to repeat the noun—e.g. "She told her **mother** that the **mother's** hairdryer was broken." In this case, however, there is a better way to avoid the ambiguity of the pronoun, namely by putting the sentence in direct discourse: "She told her mother, 'Your hairdryer is broken'" or "She told her mother, 'My hairdryer is broken.'"

The boldfaced words in the first four examples above are instances of redundancy or tautology (needless repetition of the same idea in different words). **Fellow** and **colleague, surrounding** and **environment, impending** and **eventually happen** are examples of repetitions of the same idea in different words. In the first two instances, drop the first boldfaced word; in the third, drop the whole **that** clause. In the fourth example, the phrase **in Larry's mind** is superfluous (where else does one think but in the mind?). Say simply, **Larry thinks, 'I have never met anyone so absorbed in himself.'**

Repetition of key words can be an effective means of achieving coherence (see **51,** dealing with paragraph coherence, in the next section). What you are here being cautioned about is the redundant and therefore unnecessary expression of words and ideas.

48

Avoid mixed metaphors.

Examples of mixed metaphors:

1 Sarty finally comes to the point where his inner turmoil reaches its **zenith** and **stagnates in a pool** of lethargy.

2 In "The Dead," James Joyce uses small talk as an effective **weapon** to **illustrate** his thesis.

3 He tried to **scale the wall** of indifference between them but found that he couldn't **burrow** through it.

4 For as long as Poe could remember, a **shadow** of guilt **hovered** over his head.

5 Billy was **living in a dream world** that was **wrapped up in his thoughts.**

A mixed metaphor is the result of a writer's failure to keep a consistent image in his mind. All metaphors are based on the perceived likenesses between two things that exist in a different order of being—as for instance between a *man* and a *greyhound* ("The lean shortstop is a greyhound when he runs the bases"), *fame* and a *spur* ("Fame is the spur to ambition"), *mail* and an *avalanche* ("The mail buried the staff under an avalanche of complaints"). Whenever any detail is incompatible with one or other of the terms of the analogy, the metaphor is said to be "mixed."

Zenith, as in the first example above, connotes something skyrocketing, and therefore that detail is incompatible with the detail of stagnation. It is also difficult to reconcile the notion of **turmoil** with a **stagnant pool;** turmoil connotes violent movement, but a pool is static.

A **weapon** is not used to **illustrate** something. If one were climbing **(scaling)** a wall, one could not dig **(burrow)** through it at the same time. And anyone who has ever observed a **shadow** knows that it never **hovers** over a person's head. There is a similar confusion of images in the fifth example above: Billy is living *in* a dream world, but that dream world is, in turn, wrapped up in Billy's thoughts.

Forming and maintaining a clear picture of the notion one is attempting to express figuratively will ensure a consistent metaphor.

49

Consider whether an active verb would be preferable to a passive verb.

Examples of questionable use of the passive voice:

1 Money **was borrowed** by the couple so that they could pay off all their bills.
2 His love for her **is shown** by his accepting her story and by his remaining at her side when she is in trouble.
3 From these recurrent images of hard, resistant metals, it **can be inferred** by us that he was a mechanical, heartless person.
4 Talking incessantly, he **was overwhelmed** by the girl.

The passive voice of the verb is a legitimate and useful part of the English language. A sentence using a passive verb as its predicate is a different but synonymous way of expressing the thought conveyed by a sentence using an active verb. The basic formula for a sentence using an active-verb construction is as follows:

NOUN PHRASE₁	+	VERB	+	NOUN PHRASE₂
The judge		**pronounced**		**the verdict**

The formula for transforming that active-verb construction into a passive-verb construction is as follows:

NOUN PHRASE$_2$	+	AUXILIARY	+	VERB (past participle form)	+	**by**	+	NOUN PHRASE$_1$

The verdict   **was**   **pronounced**   **by**   **the judge**

Notice the changes that have taken place in the second sentence: (1) Noun Phrase$_1$ and Noun Phrase$_2$ have switched positions, and (2) two words have been added, the auxiliary **was** and the preposition **by.** Although the second sentence expresses the same thought as the first sentence, it is longer, by two words, than the first sentence.

If the use of a passive verb is questionable, it is questionable only stylistically; that is, one can question the *choice* of a passive verb rather than an active verb in a particular instance. When someone does question the use of the passive verb, he is merely asking the writer to consider whether the sentence would not be more emphatic, more economical, less awkward, and somehow "neater" if he used an active verb. Challenged to consider the options available in a particular case, the writer still has the privilege of making the choice that seems better to him.

The writers of the first three sample sentences above should consider whether their sentences would be improved by the use of an active verb, as in these revisions:

1 The couple **borrowed** money so that they could pay off all their bills.
2 He **shows** his love for her by accepting her story and by remaining at her side when she is in trouble.

3 From these recurrent images of hard, resistant metals, we **can infer** that he was a mechanical, heartless person.

The writer of the first sentence might argue that he wanted to give special emphasis to **money,** and so he made **money** the subject of the sentence and put the word in the emphatic lead-off position in the sentence (**money was borrowed** . . .). A writer can also justify his use of a passive verb when he does not know the agent of an action or prefers not to reveal the agent or considers it unnecessary to indicate the agent, as in the sentence ''The story was reported to all the newspapers.''

Dangling verbals often result from the use of a passive-verb construction in the main clause (see **25** on dangling verbals). The writer of the fourth sentence in the examples above **(Talking incessantly, he was overwhelmed by the girl)** may not have a choice available to him. The context of that sentence suggests that the lead-off participial phrase **(talking incessantly)** may be dangling—that is, that it was not the boy **(he)** but the girl who was talking incessantly. If that is the case, the writer may not choose the passive verb instead of the active verb; he *must* use the active verb:

4 Talking incessantly, the girl overwhelmed him.

Paragraphing

One way to regard paragraphing is to view it as a system of punctuating stages of thought presented in units larger than the word and the sentence. Paragraphing is a means of alerting readers to a shift of focus in the development of the main idea of the whole discourse. It marks off for the reader's convenience the discrete but related parts of the whole discourse. How paragraphing facilitates reading would be made dramatically evident if a whole discourse were written or printed—as ancient manuscripts once were—in a single, unbroken block.

Like punctuation and mechanics, paragraphing is a feature only of the written language. Some linguists claim that speakers of connected discourse signal their "paragraphs" by pauses and by shifts in the tone of their voice. (The next time you hear a speech being delivered from a written text, see if you can detect when the speaker shifts to another paragraph of his manuscript.) But speakers are not conscious—especially in extemporaneous stretches of talk—of paragraphing the stream of sound as writers must be when they are writing their manuscripts.

The typographical device most commonly used to mark off paragraphs is *indentation*. The first line of each new para-

Paragraphing

graph starts several spaces (usually five or six spaces on the typewriter) from the left-hand margin. Another convention for marking paragraphs in printed texts is the block system: beginning every line at the left-hand margin but leaving double or triple spacing between paragraphs.

In this section, only three aspects of the paragraph are treated: unity, coherence, and adequate development. The traditional means of developing the central idea of a paragraph are mentioned in the section on adequate development, but they are not discussed at length as they are in most of the rhetoric texts. However, if writers take care of unity, coherence, and adequate development, they will be attending to the three most persistent and common problems that beset the composition of written paragraphs.

50

Preserve the unity of the paragraph.

Examples of paragraphs lacking unity:

1 The eminence of Samuel Johnson inclines modern scholars to study his thoughts and opinions. His multifarious knowledge intrigued his contemporaries. Although he manifested his interest in the drama by editing Shakespeare, he did not enjoy the theater. He was envious too of his former pupil David Garrick, the greatest actor of the eighteenth century.

2 "The Cradle Song" from the *Songs of Innocence* has internal rhyme. In this poem, the child is quiet and happy. It has a heavenly image, and throughout the poem, the mother sheds tears of joy. It has a persona—that is, one who speaks for the poet—who is naive and innocent. The poem "Infant Sorrow" contrasts with "The Cradle Song," and this contrast is very distinct. One can see a screaming and devilish child. The piping

is a harsh sound, and the child, who's against restrictions, is looking back and realizing that there is no paradise on earth.

3 Dr. Rockwell let his feelings be known on only one subject: the administration. He felt that the administrative system was outdated. Abolishing grades, giving the student a voice in administration, and revamping the curriculum were three steps he felt should be taken to improve the system. Dr. Rockwell taught in this manner. In class, a mysterious aura surrounded him. He was "hip" to what was going on, but he preferred to hear the members of the class rather than himself. He was quiet and somewhat shy. His eyes caught everything that went on in class. His eyes generated a feeling of understanding.

The principle governing paragraph unity is that a paragraph should develop a single topic or thesis, which is often, but not always, announced in a topic sentence. Every sentence in the paragraph should contribute in some way to the development of that single idea. If the writer introduces other ideas into the paragraph, he will violate the unity of the paragraph and disorient the reader.

In a sense, all three of the sample paragraphs discuss a single idea or topic: the first one talks about Samuel Johnson; the second one talks about William Blake's poetry; the third one talks about a teacher, Dr. Rockwell. But in another sense, all three paragraphs present a confusing mixture of unrelated ideas.

The first sentence of the first sample paragraph, which has the air of being a "topic sentence," talks about what Samuel Johnson means to modern scholars. Instead of the second sentence going on to develop that idea, it mentions what Dr. Johnson meant to his contemporaries. The third sentence talks about his attitude toward the drama and the theater. The fourth sentence mentions his envy of his former pupil David Garrick. What we have in this paragraph is four topics. A

Paragraphing

whole paragraph or a whole paper could be devoted to the development of each of these four topics, but here they are packed into a single paragraph.

We have observed that the second sample paragraph has a certain unity: each sentence is saying something about a poem by William Blake. But notice that the paragraph talks about *two* poems by Blake. Even though the paragraph is about two poems, however, we could still detect some unity in the paragraph if we viewed it as developing a contrast between two poems by the same author. But even if we were generous enough to concede that much unity to the paragraph, it would be difficult for us to perceive a unifying theme among the many disparate things said about the two poems.

The third sample paragraph also has a certain unity: each sentence in the paragraph is talking about the teacher, Dr. Rockwell. And there is a tight unity in the first three sentences: each of these sentences talks about Dr. Rockwell's attitude toward the administration. But with the fourth sentence of the paragraph, the writer introduces another and unrelated topic: a description of how Dr. Rockwell conducted himself in the classroom. If the writer had broken up this stretch of prose into two paragraphs, each of the two paragraphs would have had its own unity.

A paragraph will have unity, will have "oneness," if every sentence in it has an obvious bearing on the development of a single topic. If the writer senses that he has shifted to the discussion of another topic, he should begin another paragraph.

51

Compose the paragraph so that it reads coherently.

Examples of incoherent paragraphs:

1 The first stanza of "The Echoing Green" does not correspond with any other poem by Blake. The glory of nature's beauty is presented in vivid details. Emotional intensity is the overall effect of the poem. Blake resents the mechanization which has been brought about by the Industrial Revolution. The rhythm of the verses contributes to the meditative mood.

2 The preceding account illustrates all the frustrations that a beginning golfer experiences. The dominant philosophy is that the golfer who looks the best plays the best. He complicates the game by insisting on perfection the first time he sets foot on the course. More time and money are spent on clothes and equipment than on the most important aspect, skill. Winning is the only goal. Where is the idea of recreation? Try playing without a caddy sometime, and see how much exercise you get.

3 After the program has been written, each line is punched onto a card. The deck of cards is known as the "program source deck." The next step is to load the program compiler into the computer. The compiler is a program written in machine language for a particular computer, which reads the source deck and performs a translation of the program language into machine language. The machine language, in the form of instructions, is punched onto cards. This machine-language deck of cards is known as the "object deck." After the object deck has been punched, the programmer is then able to execute his program. The program is run by loading the object deck into the computer. The run of the program marks the end of the second step.

Paragraphing

Coherence is that quality which makes it easy for a reader to *follow* a writer's train of thought as it moves from sentence to sentence and from paragraph to paragraph. It facilitates reading because it ensures that the reader will be able to detect the relationships of the parts. It also reflects the clear thinking of the writer because it results from the writer's arrangement of his thoughts in some kind of perceivable order and from his use of those verbal devices that help to stitch thoughts together. In short, as the roots of the Latin word suggest (*co,* "together," + *haerēre,* "to stick"), coherence helps the parts of a discourse "stick together."

Here are some ways in which to achieve coherence in a paragraph (not all of these devices, of course, have to be used in every paragraph):

   (a)   Repeat key words from sentence to sentence or use recognizable synonyms for key words.

   (b)   Use pronouns for key nouns. (Because a pronoun gets its meaning from the noun to which it refers, it is by its very nature one of those verbal devices that help to stitch sentences together.)

   (c)   Use demonstrative adjectives, "pointing words" (**this** statement, **that** plan, **these** developments, **those** disasters).

   (d)   Use conjunctive adverbs, "thought-connecting words" **(however, moreover, also, nevertheless, therefore, thus, subsequently, indeed, then, accordingly).**

   (e)   Arrange the sequence of sentences in some kind of perceivable order (for instance, a **time order,** as in a narrative of what happened or in an explanation of how to do something; a **space order,** as in the description of a physical object or a scene; a **logical order,** such as cause to effect, effect to cause, general to particular, particular to general, whole to part, familiar to unfamiliar).

The third of the sample paragraphs above attempts to describe computer programming, a process that most readers would find difficult to follow because it is complicated and unfamiliar. But the process will be doubly baffling to readers if it is not described coherently. What makes this description of computer programming doubly difficult for the reader to follow is that the writer is doing two things at once: (1) designating the chronological sequence of steps in the process, and (2) defining the technical terms used in the description of the process. It would have been better if the writer had devoted one paragraph to defining such terms as **program source deck, compiler, program language, machine language, object deck.** Then he could have devoted another paragraph exclusively to the description of the process of "running a program"—first you do this, then you do that, after that you do this, etc. In the present paragraph, the reader gets lost because he is kept bouncing back and forth between definition of the terms and description of the process.

It is more difficult to suggest ways of revising the first two sample paragraphs; they are so incoherent that it is almost impossible to discover what the principal points were that the writers wanted to put across in them. If we could confer with the writers and ask each what the main idea of his paragraph was, we could then advise him about which of the sentences contributed to the development of that idea (and which sentences had to be dropped because they threatened the unity of the paragraph), about the order of the sentences in the paragraph, and about the verbal devices that would help to knit the sentences together.

Coherence is a difficult writing skill to master, but until the writer acquires at least a measure of that skill, he will continue to be frustrated in his efforts to communicate with

Paragraphing

others on paper. He must learn how to compose paragraphs so that the sequence of thoughts flows smoothly, easily, and logically from sentence to sentence. He must provide those bridges or links that will allow the reader to pass from sentence to sentence without being puzzled about the relationship of what is said in one sentence to what is said in the next sentence. Note how a skillful writer like Thomas Babington Macaulay stitches his sentences together by repeating key words and by using pronouns, connecting words and phrases, and parallel structures:

> It will be seen that we do not consider Bacon's ingenious analysis of the inductive method as a very useful performance. Bacon was not, as we have already said, the inventor of the inductive method. He was not even the person who first analyzed the inductive method correctly, though he undoubtedly analyzed it more minutely than any who preceded him. He was not the person who first showed that by the inductive method alone new truth could be discovered. But he was the person who first turned the minds of speculative men, long occupied in verbal disputes, to the discovery of new and useful truth; and by doing so, he at once gave to the inductive method an importance and dignity which had never belonged to it. He was not the maker of that road; he was not the discoverer of that road; he was not the person who first surveyed and mapped that road. But he was the person who first called the public attention to an inexhaustible mine of wealth, which had been utterly neglected and which was accessible by that road alone. By doing so, he caused that road, which had previously been trodden only by peasants and higglers, to be frequented by a higher class of travellers.

52

Paragraphs should be adequately developed.

Examples of inadequately developed paragraphs:

1 Wilfred Owen combines many types of imagery to get his point across. Most of his imagery is either ironic or sentimental.

2 The young people now growing up in this drug-oriented atmosphere should be made aware of the disadvantages of their indulging in drugs, just as the young people of the previous generation were cautioned about the disadvantages of their engaging in premarital sex. In both cases, responsibility for one's actions is the chief lesson to be taught.

3 The other ways in which these two men differ were that Richard was content with his life, while the Baron was bored with his. Richard was once married, while the Baron was never married but had a son as a result of an affair.

Generally, one- and two-sentence paragraphs are not effective, except for purposes of emphasis, transition, or dialogue.

The preceding one-sentence paragraph can be justified on the grounds that the writer wanted to give special emphasis to a principle by setting it aside in a paragraph by itself. Separate paragraphing for emphasis is a graphic device comparable to italicizing (underlining) a word or a phrase in a sentence for emphasis. Set aside in a paragraph by itself, an important idea achieves a prominence that would be missed if the idea were merged with other ideas in the same paragraph.

A one- or two-sentence paragraph can also be used to mark or announce a transition from one major division of a discourse to the next major division. Transitional paragraphs facilitate reading because they orient the reader, reminding him of what has been discussed and alerting him to what is

Paragraphing

going to be discussed. They are like signposts marking the major stages of a journey. Note how the following two-sentence paragraph helps to orient the reader:

> After presenting his Introduction to *Songs of Experience,* William Blake apparently feels that his readers have been sufficiently warned about their earthly predicament. Let us see now how he uses the poems in *Songs of Experience* to illustrate what the people might do to solve their problems.

One of the conventions in printing is that in representing dialogue in a story we should begin a new paragraph every time the speaker changes. A paragraph of dialogue can be one sentence long or ten sentences long (any number of sentences really). A paragraph of dialogue may also consist of only a phrase or a single word:

> "It's a beautiful day, isn't it?" Melvin asked.
> "Yup," Hank muttered.
> "Remember yesterday?"
> "Yup."
> "I thought it would never stop raining."
> "Me too."

Once an exchange like that gets going, the author can dispense with the identifying tags, because the separate paragraphing will mark the shift in speakers.

But except for the purposes of emphasis, transition, or dialogue, a one- or a two-sentence paragraph can rarely be justified; it is almost a contradiction in terms. There can be little if any development in a single sentence. In a two-sentence paragraph, one of the sentences is likely to be the topic sentence; the remaining sentence is hardly enough to develop the topic idea adequately.

Judgment about whether a paragraph is adequately developed is, of course, a relative matter. Because some ideas need more development than others, no one can say absolutely how many sentences a paragraph needs to be satis-factorily developed. But a topic sentence does set at least a general commitment that a writer must fulfill. When the writer of the first sample paragraph above says, in what is obviously the topic sentence, **Wilfred Owen combines many types of imagery to get his point across,** we have every right to expect that he will specify and discuss several, if not many, types of imagery. But when he develops that topic idea with only one sentence, which is only slightly less general than his first sentence, we can feel quite safe in pronouncing that *this* paragraph is inadequately developed. An obvious way for him to develop the ideas contained in his two sentences is to cite examples, first of ironic imagery, then of sentimental imagery. To flesh out the mere cataloguing of these exam-ples, he could go on to show how these images help the author "get his point across."

Even if the second sample paragraph were a summary paragraph that followed a paragraph (or several paragraphs) in which the writer had discussed the disadvantages of in-dulging in drugs, the reader could reasonably expect the writer to say something more about the notion presented in his second sentence. What kind of legal or moral responsibil-ities does an addict have to himself? What kind of responsi-bilities does he have to his family and to society in general? Once an addict has been "hooked," can he still be held responsible for his actions? What are the consequences, for himself and for society, of his refusing to be responsible for his actions? These questions suggest ways in which the writer might have expanded his thinly developed paragraph.

The writer of the third sample paragraph might have been able to justify his two-sentence paragraph if there were only *two* "other ways" in which Richard Harenger and the Baron Mordiane differed. But if you knew the stories he was dis-cussing (Somerset Maugham's "The Treasure" and Guy de

Paragraphing

Maupassant's "Douchoux") and if you had seen the differences he discussed later on in the paper, you would realize that there were other, even more significant, differences that he might have mentioned and discussed in this paragraph. The topic sentence commits the writer to developing an extensive contrast between the two characters; by citing only two rather superficial differences, he has clearly not delivered on his commitment.

A topic sentence will suggest how long a paragraph has to be in order to create an impression of being adequately developed. Some sentences commit a writer to more development than others. A sentence like "There was only one way in which Julie could rouse John out of bed in the morning" obviously entails less development than a sentence like "There were several ways in which Julie could rouse John out of bed in the morning." A writer must train himself to look at a topic sentence and see what it commits him to do in the paragraph. Then of course he must have resources at his command so that he can fulfill his commitment. Sometimes he can draw on examples or illustrations to expand his paragraph; sometimes he can develop his topic idea by stating it in a variety of different ways; sometimes he can expand his paragraph by comparison or contrast or by analogy or by an anecdote; or he can trace out the causes or the consequences of what he is talking about. Invention, discovering something to say, is of course the crucial part of the composition process. Thinly developed paragraphs are the result of a writer's not thinking enough about his subject to discover what he already knows about it and what he needs to find out about it in order to develop it. Almost invariably he knows more about the idea stated in a topic sentence than he puts down in a one- or two-sentence paragraph. He must be made aware, or must force himself to become aware, of all that he really knows about the topic idea.

Punctuation

Graphic punctuation, which is the only kind dealt with in this section, is a feature of the written language exclusively. For the written language, it performs the kinds of functions that intonation (pitch, stress, pause, and juncture) performs for the spoken language. Punctuation and intonation can be considered as part of the grammar of a language because they join with other grammatical devices (word order, inflections, and function words) to help convey meaning. If writers would regard punctuation as an integral—and often indispensable—part of the expressive system of a language, they might cease to think of it as just another nuisance imposed on them by editors and English teachers.

In *Structural Essentials of English* (New York: Harcourt Brace Jovanovich, 1956), Harold Whitehall has neatly summarized the four main functions of graphic punctuation:

☐ **For LINKING parts of sentences and words.**
   semicolon
   colon
   dash
   hyphen (for words only)

Punctuation

☐ For SEPARATING sentences and parts of sentences.
 period
 question mark
 exclamation point
 comma

☐ For ENCLOSING parts of sentences.

 pair of commas
 pair of dashes
 pair of parentheses
 pair of brackets
 pair of quotation marks

☐ For INDICATING omissions.

 apostrophe (e.g. **don't, we'll, it's, we've**)
 period (e.g. abbreviations, **Mrs., U.S., A.H. Robinson**)
 dash (e.g. **John R--, D--n!**)
 triple periods (. . . to indicate omitted words in a quotation)

Punctuation is strictly a convention. There is no reason in the nature of things why the mark **?** should be used in English to indicate a question. The Greek language, for instance, uses **;** (what we call a semicolon) to mark questions. Nor is there any reason in the nature of things why the single comma should be a separating device rather than a linking device. Usage has established the distinctive functions of the various marks of punctuation. And although styles of punctuation have changed somewhat from century to century and even from country to country, the conventions of punctuation set forth in the following section are the prevailing conventions in the United States in the second half of the twentieth century. Although publishers of newspapers, magazines, and books often have style manuals that prescribe, for their own editors and writers, a style of punctuation that may differ in some particulars from the prevailing conventions, the writer who observes the conventions of punctuation set forth in this section can rest assured that he is following the predominant system in the United States.

60

Put a comma in front of the coordinating conjunction that joins the independent clauses of a compound sentence.

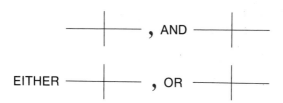

Examples:

1 He disliked this kind of cruel humor, yet when he met the actress at a dinner party, he teased her unmercifully.

2 Alice's embarrassment amused Julian, so he deliberately pursued the conversation with the Dirty Old Man across the aisle.

3 The decision about whether to attend college should be left entirely to the child, and his parents should make every effort to reconcile themselves to his decision.

4 It was snowing outside, and in the building William felt safe.

5 Nick relates all the happenings in his own words, and sometimes his own interpretations of another character or situation are revealed.

6 Either the senators will reject the proposal, or they will modify it in such a way as to make it innocuous.

Pairs of independent clauses joined by one of the coordinating conjunctions **(and, but, or, nor, for, yet, so)** or by one of the correlative conjunctions **(either . . . or, neither . . . nor, not only . . . but)** are the only coordinate pairs that should be separated with a comma (see **62**). The reason why this convention developed is that in many situations, the absence of the comma could lead to an initial misreading of the sentence, as in the third example above or in a sentence like this: "He returned the book for his mother refused to pay any more fines." In the latter sentence, it would be quite natural for us to read **for** as a preposition. Consequently, we might initially read the sentence this way: **He returned the book for his mother** . . . but when we came to the verb **refused,** we would realize that we had misread the syntax of the sentence and would have to back up and reread the sentence. If you read the third, fourth, and fifth sample sentences *without the comma,* you will be aware of the possibility of a misreading of those sentences. A comma placed before the coordinating conjunction that joins the two parts of a compound sentence will prevent such misreadings.

Some handbooks authorize you to omit this separating comma if three conditions prevail: (1) if the two clauses of the compound sentence are short, (2) if there is no punctuation within either of the two clauses, and (3) if there is no chance that the syntax will be misread. (The following sentence satisfies these three conditions: "He said he would go and he did.") However, if you *invariably* insert a comma before the coordinating conjunction that joins the independent clauses of a compound sentence, you never have to pause to consider whether there is a chance that your sentence will be misread, and you can be confident that your sentence will always be read correctly the first time.

The safest practice is *always* to insert the comma before

the coordinating conjunction that joins the main clauses of a compound sentence.

61

Introductory words, phrases, or clauses shoud be separated from the main (independent) clause by a comma.

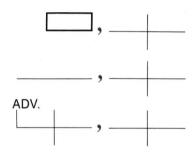

Examples:

1 Underneath, the papers were scorched.
   (*introductory word*)

2 I tiptoed into the house. Inside, the front room looked as though it had been recently finger-painted by a group of three-year-olds.
   (*introductory word*)

3 In addition to the logical errors, Doris had made several miscalculations in addition and subtraction.
   (*introductory prepositional phrase*)

4 As we went by, the church revealed all of its redbrick Georgian elegance.
   (*introductory adverbial clause*)

Punctuation

5 After hurriedly gathering **,** the crowd decided to rush the gates.

(introductory verbal phrase)

6 Although he vehemently protested **,** the violence was not as destructive as he predicted it would be.

(introductory adverbial clause)

The reason why this convention developed is that the comma facilitates the reading of the sentence and often prevents an initial misreading. Without the "protective" comma in the six examples above, the syntax of those sentences would probably be misread on the first reading. If the comma were left out, most readers would probably read the sentences in this way:

1 Underneath the papers . . .

2 Inside the front room . . .

3 In addition to the logical errors [that] Doris had made . . .

4 As we went by the church . . .

5 After hurriedly gathering the crowd . . .

6 Although he vehemently protested the violence . . .

The insertion of a comma after the introductory element prevents that kind of misreading.

Even in those instances, however, where there is little or no chance of an initial misreading, the insertion of a comma after the introductory word, phrase, or clause will facilitate the reading of the sentence. Put a comma after the introductory word, phrase, or clause in the following sentences, and see whether it isn't easier to read the sentences:

Besides the crowd wasn't impressed by his flaming oratory.

Having failed to impress the crowd with his flaming oratory he tried another tactic.

After he saw that his flaming oratory had not impressed the crowd he tried another tactic.

If a writer *always* inserts a comma after an introductory word, phrase, or clause, he will not have to consider each time whether it would be safe to omit the comma, and he can be confident that his sentence will not be misread.

62

Pairs of words, phrases, or dependent clauses joined by one of the coordinating conjunctions should not be separated with a comma.

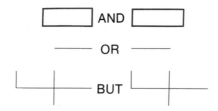

Examples:

1 The **mother AND** the **father appeared** in court **AND testified** about their son's activities.

   (*two nouns and two verbs joined by **and***)

2 There was nothing they could do **to prevent** the gas attack **OR to protect** themselves against the gas once it had been released.

   (*two infinitive phrases joined by **or***)

3 The men **who are able to work BUT who are not willing to work** will not be eligible to receive monthly welfare checks.

   (*two adjective clauses joined by **but***)

The principle behind this convention is that what has been joined by one means (the coordinating conjunction) should not then be separated by another means (the comma,

Punctuation

a separating device). The function of the coordinating conjunction is to join units of equal rank (e.g. nouns with nouns, verbs with verbs, prepositional phrases with prepositional phrases, participial phrases with participial phrases, adjective clauses with adjective clauses, adverb clauses with adverb clauses). Once pairs of coordinate units have been joined by the conjunction, it makes no sense to separate them with a comma, like this: **the mother, and the father.** If a coordinating conjunction is not used to join the pair, a comma should be used to separate the pair, like this: "the tall, handsome man" (but not "the tall, and handsome man").

One exception to this convention, as in **60,** is a pair of *independent* clauses joined by a coordinating conjunction. According to **60**, a comma should be inserted before the coordinating conjunction, because in this particular structure the omission of the comma could lead—and often does lead—to an initial misreading of the sentence. But there are almost no instances where the use of a comma would prevent the misreading of pairs of words, phrases, or dependent clauses joined by a coordinating conjunction. As a matter of fact, if the first sample sentence were punctuated in this fashion, it would be harder to read: **The mother, and the father appeared in court, and testified about the son's activities.** If some subtle distinction in meaning were effected by these commas, or if the clarity of the sentence were threatened by the absence of the commas, the writer might be able to justify the use of commas in this sentence; but neither of those conditions seems to prevail here. The commas would only confuse the reader.

Another exception to this convention occurs in the case of suspended structures, as in the following sentence:

> This account of an author's struggles with, and his anxieties about, his writing fascinated me.

The phrases *struggles with* and *anxieties about* are called "suspended structures" because they are left "hanging" until the noun phrase *his writing,* which completes them grammatically, occurs. If the writer of this sentence could have written "This account of an author's struggles and anxieties about his writing fascinated me," he would not, in accord with the directions in **62**, have put a comma in front of the *and* that joins the pair of nouns *struggles* and *anxieties.* But he saw that although the preposition *about* fitted idiomatically with *anxieties,* it did not fit idiomatically with *struggles.* So he was faced with two choices. He could complete both structures and write "This account of an author's struggles with his writing and his anxieties about his writing fascinated me." But preferring to avoid the repetition of *his writing,* he chose to use suspended structures, and he alerted the reader to the suspended structures by putting a comma after *with* and after *about.* Inserting a comma before the conjunction *and,* which joins the two phrases, makes it easier for us to read the sentence.

Unless you have some compelling reason, like protecting the clarity of the sentence or facilitating the reading of a sentence, do not separate with a comma pairs of parallel elements that have been joined with a coordinating conjunction.

63

**Use a comma to separate a series of coordinate
words, phrases, or clauses.**

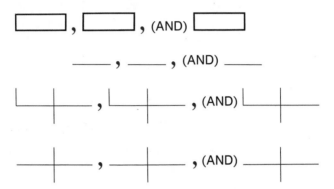

(The parentheses around **and** in the diagrams above indicate
that the coordinating conjunction between the last two members of a series may sometimes be dispensed with. For instance, the phrasing **The tall, robust, gray-haired soldier
rose to speak** is stylistically preferable to **The tall, robust,
and gray-haired soldier rose to speak**.)

Examples:

1 Could he cope with the challenges posed by war, poverty,
 pollution, and crime?

 (*a series of nouns*)

2 He would have to terminate the war, alleviate the plight of the
 poor, arrest the contamination of the environment, and hobble
 the criminal.

 (*series of infinitive phrases, with **to** understood in the last three
 members of the series*)

3 If he is willing to work hard **,** if he is resourceful enough to formulate sensible policies **,** if he subordinates his own interests to the interests of the community, he could rescue the nation from the despair that now prevails.

(*series of adverb clauses*)

4 He wanted to save the nation **,** he knew he could save it **,** and eventually he did save it.

(*series of independent clauses*)

Whereas the convention stated in **62** says that *pairs* of coordinate words, phrases, or clauses should not be separated with a comma, the convention governing a *series* of coordinate words, phrases, or clauses says that these units should be separated with a comma. (A **series** is to be understood as a sequence of **three or more** coordinate units.) Built on the principle of parallelism (see **27**), the series always involves words, phrases, or clauses of a similar kind. So a series should never couple nouns with adjectives, prepositional phrases with infinitive phrases, adjective clauses with adverb clauses, etc.

The convention that will be recommended here follows this formula: **a, b, and c.** Another acceptable formula for the series is **a, b and c**—where no comma is used between the last two members of the series when they are joined by a coordinating conjunction. The formula **a, b, and c** is adopted here because the alternative formula **(a, b and c)** sometimes leads to ambiguity. Consider the following example, which uses the **a, b and c** formula:

Please send me a gross each of **the red, green, blue, orange and black ties.**

The shipping clerk who received that order might wonder whether five gross of ties (red, green, blue, orange, black)

Punctuation

were being ordered or only four gross (red, green, blue, orange-and-black). If five gross were being ordered, a comma after **orange** would specify the order unequivocally; if four gross were being ordered, hyphens should have been used to signify the combination of colors.

A more common instance of the ambiguity sometimes created by the use of the **a, b and c** formula is one like the following:

He appealed to **the administrators, the deans and the chairmen.**

In this sentence, it is not clear whether he appealed to three different groups (administrators, deans, chairmen—a meaning that would have been clearly indicated by the **a, b, and c** formula) or to only one group, **administrators,** who are then specified in the double appositive **deans and chairmen.**

Since there is never any chance of ambiguity if you use the **a, b, and c** formula, you would be well advised to adopt this option for punctuating a series.

64

Nonrestrictive adjective clauses should be enclosed with a pair of commas.

Examples:

1 My oldest brother**,** **who is a chemist,** was hurt in an accident last week.
2 The shopkeeper caters only to American tourists**, who usually**

have enough money to buy what they want , and to aristo-cratic families.

3 Norman Mailer's book **, which most reviewers considered juvenile in its pronouncements ,** was severely panned by the women's liberation groups.

4 The townsmen threaten the strangers **,** who are looking at the young girl.

A nonrestrictive adjective clause is one that supplies infor-mation about the noun that it modifies but information that is not needed to identify the particular person, place, or thing that is being talked about. (The four **that** clauses in the previous sentence, for instance, are **restrictive** adjective clauses—clauses that identify the nouns that they modify.)

In the case of the first example above, the adjective clause **who is a chemist** supplies additional information about **my oldest brother,** but this information is not needed to identify which of the brothers was hurt in the accident, because the adjective **oldest** sufficiently identifies the brother being talked about.

One test to determine whether an adjective clause is nonrestrictive or not is to read the sentence without the adjective clause, and if the particular person, place, or thing being talked about is sufficiently identified by what is left, the adjective clause can be considered nonrestrictive—and, ac-cording to the convention, should be marked off with enclos-ing commas. If, for instance, you were to drop the adjective clause from the first example and say **My oldest brother was hurt in an accident last week,** your readers would not have to ask, "Which one of your brothers was hurt?" The brother is specified by the adjective **oldest,** since there can be only one oldest brother. The clause **who is a chemist** merely supplies some additional but nonessential information about the oldest brother.

Punctuation

Another test to determine whether an adjective clause is nonrestrictive or not is the **intonation** test. Read these two sentences aloud:

He caters to American tourists, who have enough money to buy what they want, and to aristocratic families.

He caters to American tourists who have enough money to buy what they want and to aristocratic families.

In reading the first sentence aloud, native speakers of the language would pause briefly after the words **tourists** and **want** (that is, in the places where the commas are in the written form of the sentence) and would lower the pitch of their voices slightly in enunciating the clause **who have enough money to buy what they want.** In reading the second sentence aloud, native speakers would read right through without a pause and would not lower the pitch of their voices in reading the adjective clause. In writing, it makes a *significant* difference whether the adjective clause in that sentence is or is not enclosed with commas. With the enclosing commas, the sentence means this: He caters to American tourists (who, incidentally, usually have enough money to buy what they want) and to aristocratic families. Without the enclosing commas, the sentence means this: He caters only to those American tourists who have enough money to buy what they want (he doesn't cater to American tourists who don't have enough money to buy) and to aristocratic families. Likewise, the presence of the comma before the adjective clause in the fourth sample sentence indicates that the townsmen threaten *all* the strangers, because all of them are looking at the young girl. Without the comma before the **who** clause, the sentence would mean that the townsmen threaten *only* those strangers who are looking at the young girl. So whether the adjective clause is marked off with commas or not makes a real difference in the *meaning* of the sentence.

64 Comma, Nonrestrictive

There are some instances in which the adjective clause is almost invariably nonrestrictive:

(a) Where the antecedent is a **proper noun,** the adjective clause is usually nonrestrictive:

Martin Chuzzlewit, who is a character in Dicken's novel, . . .

New York City, which has the largest urban population in the United States, . . .

The College of William and Mary, which was founded in 1693, . . .

(b) Where, in the nature of things, there could be **only one such** person, place, or thing, the adjective clause is usually nonrestrictive:

My mother, who is now forty-six years old, . . .

Their birthplace, which is Jamestown, . . .

His fingerprints, which are on file in Washington, . . .

(c) Where the identity of the antecedent has been clearly established by the **previous context,** the adjective clause is usually nonrestrictive:

My brother, who has hazel eyes, . . . (where it is clear from the context that you have only one brother)

The book, which never made the bestseller list, . . . (where the previous sentence has identified the particular book being talked about)

Such revolutions, which never enlist the sympathies of the majority of the people, . . . (where the kinds of revolutions being talked about have been specified in the previous sentences or paragraphs)

Which is the usual relative pronoun that introduces nonrestrictive adjective clauses. **That** is the more common relative pronoun used in restrictive adjective clauses. **Who** (or its

Punctuation

inflected forms **whose** and **whom**) is the usual relative pronoun when the antecedent is a person; **that,** however, may
also be used when the antecedent is a person and the clause
is restrictive: either "the men whom I admire" or "the men
that I admire."

65

**Restrictive adjective clauses should not be marked
off with a pair of commas.**

ADJ.
(NO COMMA) └──────┼────── (NO COMMA)

Examples:

1 My brother **who graduated from college in June** was hurt in an
accident last week.

2 The poem is about a boy **who has been in Vietnam and has
rejoined his family.**

3 The city is obliged to maintain all streets, alleys, and thorough-
fares **that are in the public domain.**

A restrictive adjective clause is one that identifies the particular person, place, or thing being talked about. It "restricts"
the noun that it modifies; it "defines"—that is, "draws
boundaries around"—the noun being talked about.

In the first example above, the adjective clause **who graduated from college in June** is restrictive because it identifies, defines, designates, specifies which one of the brothers
was hurt in the accident. Unlike the nonrestrictive adjective
clause (see **64**), which merely supplies additional but nonessential information about the noun that it modifies, the

restrictive adjective clause supplies information that is needed to identify the noun being talked about.

Whether an adjective clause is restrictive or nonrestrictive makes a substantial difference in the meaning of a sentence. Consider, for instance, these two sentences:

Women who have unusually slow reflexes should be denied a driver's license.

(*restrictive—note the absence of enclosing commas around the **who** clause*)

Women, who have unusually slow reflexes, should be denied a driver's license.

(*nonrestrictive—note the enclosing commas around the **who** clause*)

The import of the first sentence is that only those women who have unusually slow reflexes should be denied a driver's license. The import of the second sentence is that *all* women should be denied a driver's license, because they have unusually slow reflexes (a claim, incidentally, that is untrue). The presence or absence of commas makes a vital difference in the meaning of the two sentences. For this reason, the punctuation of the sentences is not a matter of option or whim.

If you were speaking those two sentences aloud, your voice would do what the presence or the absence of commas does. In the first sentence, your voice would join the **who** clause with **women** by running through without a pause after **women.** In the second sentence, your voice would pause slightly after **women** and would utter the **who** clause on a slightly lower pitch than the rest of the sentence. In addition to the test of whether the adjective clause is needed to specify the noun referred to, you can use this test of intonation to discriminate restrictive and nonrestrictive clauses.

Restrictive adjective clauses modifying nonhuman nouns

Punctuation

should be introduced with the relative pronoun **that** rather than with **which:**

> Governments, which are instituted to protect the rights of men, should be responsive to the will of the people.
>
> (*nonrestrictive*)
>
> Governments that want to remain in favor with their constituents must be responsive to the will of the people.
>
> (*restrictive*)

Here is another distinctive fact about the phrasing of restrictive and nonrestrictive adjective clauses: the relative pronoun may sometimes be omitted in restrictive clauses, but it may never be omitted in nonrestrictive clauses. Note that it is impossible in English to drop the relative pronouns **who** and **whom** from the following nonrestrictive clauses:

> John, who is my dearest friend, won't drink with me.
>
> John, whom I love dearly, hardly notices me.

(In the first sentence, however, the clause **who is my dearest friend** could be reduced to an appositive phrase: **John, my dearest friend, won't drink with me.**)

In restrictive adjective clauses, we sometimes have the option of using or not using the relative pronoun:

> The man whom I love dearly hardly notices me.
>
> (*with the relative pronoun*)
>
> The man that I love dearly hardly notices me.
>
> (*with the relative pronoun*)
>
> The man I love dearly hardly notices me.
>
> (*without the relative pronoun*)

In restrictive adjective clauses like these, where the relative pronoun serves as the object of the verb of the adjective

66 Semicolon, Compound Sentence

clause, the relative pronoun may be omitted. The relative pronoun in restrictive clauses may also be omitted if it serves as the object of a preposition in the adjective clause: "The man I gave the wallet to disappeared" (here the understood **whom** or **that** serves as the object of the preposition **to**). However, the relative pronoun may *not* be omitted when the relative pronoun serves as the subject of the adjective clause:

> He who exalts himself shall be humbled.
>
> (**who** *cannot be omitted*)
>
> The money that was set aside for scholarships was squandered on roads.
>
> (**that** *cannot be omitted*)

66

If the independent clauses of a compound sentence are not joined by one of the coordinating conjunctions, they should be joined by a semicolon.

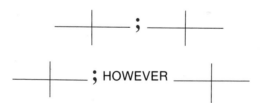

Examples:

1 This refutation is based on an appeal to reason; however, one must remember that an emotional appeal can also move people to reject an argument.

2 All the students spontaneously supported the team; they wanted to show their loyalty, even though they were disappointed with the outcome of the game.

Punctuation

3 He loved his mother **;** in fact, he practically worshiped her.

The coordinating conjunctions are **and, but, or, nor, for, yet, so.** In the absence of one of those words, the independent clauses of a compound sentence should be spliced together with a punctuation device: the semicolon.

Words and expressions like **however, therefore, then, in fact, indeed, nevertheless, consequently, thus, moreover, on the other hand, on the contrary** are not coordinating conjunctions; they are called **conjunctive adverbs.** Conjunctive adverbs provide logical links between sentences and between parts of sentences, but they do not function as grammatical splicers. Unlike coordinating conjunctions, which must always be placed *between* the two elements they join, conjunctive adverbs enjoy some freedom of movement in the sentence. In the first sample sentence above, the word **however** is placed between the two independent clauses, but evidence that this conjunctive adverb is not serving as the grammatical splicer of the two clauses is provided by the fact that **however** can be shifted to another position in the sentence: **This refutation is based on an appeal to reason; one must remember, however, that an emotional appeal can also move people to reject an argument.** The coordinating conjunction **but,** on the other hand, could occupy no other position in the sentence than *between* the end of the first clause and the beginning of the next clause.

Nor can the independent clauses of a compound sentence be joined by a comma, because the comma is a separating device, not a joining device. Compound sentences so punctuated are called **comma splices** (see **30**). As indicated in **60**, if a compound sentence is joined by one of the coordinating conjunctions, a comma should be put in front of the conjunction to mark off the end of one independent clause and the beginning of the next independent clause. But when a coordinating conjunction is not present to join the independent clauses, a semicolon must be used to join them. The semicolon serves both to mark the division between the two clauses and to join them.

It is sometimes advisable to use both a semicolon and a coordinating conjunction to join the independent clauses of a compound sentence. When the clauses are unusually long and have commas within them, a semicolon placed before the coordinating conjunction helps to demarcate the end of one clause and the beginning of the next one, as in this example:

> Struggling to salvage what was left of the semester, he pleaded with his English teacher, who was notoriously softhearted, to grant him an extension of time on his written assignments, quizzes, and class reports; **but** he forgot that, even with the best of intentions, he had only so many hours every day when he could study and only a limited reserve of energy.

The coordinating conjunction **but** serves to join the two main clauses of the compound sentence, but the use of the semicolon in addition to the conjunction makes it easier to read the sentence.

67

Whenever you use a semicolon, be sure that you have an independent clause on both sides of the semicolon.

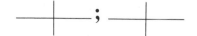

Punctuation

67 Independent Clause on Both Sides o

Examples of failure to observe this convention:

1 He played the banjo expertly **;** although he couldn't read a note of music.

2 Americans spend far too many hours as spectators of sports instead of as participants in them **;** watching meaningless drivel on television instead of spending that time reading a book.

3 The two series of poems also differ in style **;** the *Songs of Experience* being more vague and complex than the *Songs of Innocence.*

4 An industry like this benefits everyone, from the poor, for whom it creates employment **;** to the rich, who are made richer by it.

This convention is the corollary of **66**. It cautions against using the semicolon to join elements of unequal rank.

In all of the examples above, a semicolon has been used to join units of unequal rank. In all three sentences, there is an independent clause on the *left-hand* side of the semicolon; however, there is no independent clause on the *right-hand* side of the semicolon in any of those sentences.

In the first example above, there is the independent clause **He played the banjo expertly** on the left-hand side of the semicolon, but on the right-hand side of the semicolon, there is only the adverb clause **although he couldn't read a note of music.** That adverb clause belongs with, depends on, the first clause. Since it is an integral part of the first clause, it should be joined with that clause. The effect of the semicolon is to make the adverb clause part of a new clause that begins after the semicolon. But on the right-hand side of the semicolon, there is no independent clause that the subordinate, dependent adverb clause can be a part of.

The first, third, and fourth examples above can be revised by simply replacing the semicolon with a comma. The second example, however, cannot be revised by a simple change of punctuation. The writer has to supply an independent clause after the semicolon. He can supply that independent clause by adding the words **they spend far too many hours,** so that the whole clause reads, **they spend far too many hours watching meaningless drivel on television instead of spending that time reading a book.** So revised, the sentence has an independent clause on *both* sides of the semicolon.

Like the coordinating conjunction, for which it can serve as a substitute, the semicolon joins parts of equal rank. Therefore, if there is an independent clause on one side of the semicolon, there must be a balancing independent clause on the other side.

68

Use a colon after a grammatically complete lead-in sentence that formally announces a subsequent enumeration, explanation, illustration, or extended quotation.

Examples:

1 The courses I am taking this quarter are as follows : English, sociology, economics, political science, and psychology.

2 His approach works like this : after displaying his product and extolling its virtues, he asks the housewife if she has a small rug that she would like to have cleaned.

3 Examples of the diction used to evoke the horror of the scene include vivid images like these : "coughing like hags," "thick

green light," "guttering," "white eyes writhing in his face,"
"gargling from froth-corrupted lungs."

4 The reaction of the crowd signified only one thing**:** apathy.

5 (*note the use of a colon after a lead-in sentence for an extended quotation in a research paper.*)

Toward the end of the *Preface,* Dr. Johnson confessed that he abandoned his earlier expectation that his dictionary would be able to "fix the language"**:**

Those who have been persuaded to think well of my design will require that it should fix our language and put a stop to those alterations which time and chance have hitherto been suffered to make in it without opposition. With this consequence I will confess that I flattered myself for a while; but now begin to fear that I have indulged expectation which neither reason nor experience can justify.

Note that although a word, a phrase, or a clause or a series of words, phrases, or clauses can follow the colon, there must be an independent clause (a grammatically complete sentence) on the left-hand side of the colon.

In accord with this principle, you should not punctuate a sentence in this fashion:

The courses I am taking this quarter are: English, sociology, economics, political science, and psychology.

That punctuation makes no more sense than punctuating a sentence in this way:

My name is: John Adams.

In both cases, the words following the colon are needed to complete the sentence grammatically.

What distinguishes the colon from the dash as a symbolic device is that the colon throws the reader's attention *forward,* whereas the dash as a linking device throws the reader's attention *backward.* What the colon signifies is that what *follows* is a specification of what was formally announced in the clause on the left-hand side of the colon.

69

Use a dash when the word or word-group that follows it constitutes a summation, an amplification, or a reversal of what went before it.

Examples:

1 English, psychology, history, and philosophy—these were the courses I took last quarter.
2 If he was pressured, he would become sullen and close-lipped—a reaction that did not endear him to the President or to the Senate.
3 Time and time again he would admit that his critics were right, that he should have realized his mistakes, that he should have read the danger signs more accurately—and then go ahead with his original plans.

Unlike the colon, which directs the reader's attention forward, the dash usually directs the reader's attention backward. What follows the dash, when it is used as a linking device, looks back to what preceded it for the particulars or details that spell out its meaning or invest its meaning with pungency or irony.

The colon and the dash are usually not interchangeable marks of punctuation. They signal a different relationship between the word-groups that precede them and those that follow them. After much practice in writing, one develops a sense for the subtle distinction in relationships that is signaled by the punctuation in the following sentences:

The reaction of the crowd signified only one thing: apathy.

Punctuation

> The crowd clearly indicated their indifference to the provocative speech—an apathy that later came back to haunt them.

In the first sentence, the lead-in clause before the colon clearly alerts the reader to expect a specification of what is hinted at in that clause. In the second sentence, there is no such alerting of the reader in the lead-in clause; but following the dash, there is an unexpected commentary on what was said in the lead-in clause, a summary commentary that forces the reader to look backward. The colon and the single dash are both linking devices, but they signal different kinds of thought relationships between parts of the sentence.

Finally, the writer should be cautioned to avoid using the dash as a catchall mark of punctuation, one that indiscriminately substitutes for periods, commas, semicolons, etc.

70
Use a pair of dashes to enclose abrupt parenthetical elements that occur within a sentence.

— —   — —

Examples:

1 In some instances—although no one will admit it—the police overreacted to the provocation.

2 What surprised everyone when the measure came to a vote was the chairman's reluctance—indeed, downright refusal—to allow any riders to be attached to the bill.

3 One of them—let me call him Jim Prude—is clean-shaven and dresses like an Ivy Leaguer of the early 1950s.

4 Their unhappiness is due to the ease with which envy is aroused

and to the difficulty—or should I say impossibility?—of fighting against it.

5 Yet despite the similarities in their travelogues—for indeed the same trip inspired both works—the two reports differ in some key aspects.

The three devices used to set off parenthetical elements in written prose are commas, parentheses, and dashes. The kind of parenthetical element that should be enclosed with a pair of dashes is the kind that interrupts the normal syntactical flow of the sentence. What characterizes such elements in the examples above is that they abruptly arrest the normal flow of the sentence to add some qualifying or rectifying information. The rhetorical effect of the enclosing dashes is to give the parenthetical element an unusual measure of emphasis.

A pair of parentheses is another typographical device used to mark off parenthetical elements in a sentence. Enclosure within parentheses is used mainly for those elements that merely add information or identification, as in sentences like these:

> All the companies that used the service were charged a small fee (usually $500) and were required to sign a contract (an "exclusive-use" agreement).

> The manager of each franchise is expected to report monthly to NARM (National Association of Retail Merchants) and to "rotate" (take turns doing various jobs) every two weeks.

The typographical device used to set off the mildest kind of interrupting element is a pair of commas. Whether to enclose a parenthetical element with commas or with parentheses or with dashes is more a matter of stylistic choice than a matter of grammatical necessity. There are degrees of interruption and emphasis, and with practice, a writer develops an instinct

Punctuation

for knowing when to mark off parenthetical elements with commas (lowest degree of interruption and emphasis), when to mark them off with parentheses (middle degree), and when to mark them off with dashes (highest degree). Consider the degrees of interruption and emphasis in the following sentences:

> That agency, as we have since learned, reported the incident directly to the Department of Justice.

> During the postwar years (at least from 1946 to 1952), no one in the agency dared challenge a directive from higher up.

> When the order was challenged, the attorney general—some claim it was his wife—put a call through to the president.

71

A dash is made on the typewriter with two unspaced hyphens and with no space before the dash or after the dash. (In handwriting, the dash should be made slightly longer than a hyphen.)

Example:

```
He forgot--if he ever knew--the functions of
the various marks of punctuation.
```

Do not hit the spacebar on the typewriter *before* the first hyphen, *between* the first and second hyphen, or *after* the second hyphen. In short, do not hit the spacebar at all in forming the dash on the typewriter.

Avoid the following kinds of typography in forming the dash on the typewriter:

He forgot—if he ever knew—the functions of
the various marks of punctuation.

He forgot – if he ever knew – the functions of
the various marks of punctuation.

He forgot ── if he ever knew ── the functions
of the various marks of punctuation.

He forgot – – if he ever knew – – the functions of the various marks of punctuation.

Mechanics

The graphic devices dealt with in this section might be, and often are, classified as punctuation. But because such graphic devices as italics, capitalization, and numbers are not correlated—as punctuation marks are—with the intonational patterns of the spoken language, these devices are grouped in a separate section under the heading Mechanics. In the spoken language, a word printed with a capital letter is pronounced no differently from the same word printed with a lower-case letter. Nor is the italicized title of a book pronounced any differently from that same title printed without italics. (Italics used for emphasizing a word or phrase, however, do correspond to stress in the spoken language.) Even quotation marks, which one might regard as correlated with the spoken language, do not correspond to anything the voice does when it quotes direct speech.

But whether one classifies these graphic devices as punctuation or as mechanics is immaterial. What is important to remember is that these devices are part of the written language exclusively and that they facilitate the reading of that language. Most readers would have at least momentary difficulty making sense of the following string of words:

candy cane replied in the united states people use gas to refer to the liquid propellant that is called petrol in other english speaking countries

If the proper punctuation and mechanics were used with that string of words, readers would be spared the momentary difficulty:

Candy Cane replied, "In the United States, people use *gas* to refer to the liquid propellant that is called *petrol* in other English-speaking countries."

Deprived of the resources that the human voice has to clarify the meaning of a spoken utterance, the writer should be eager to use all those typographical devices that make it easier for his readers to grasp what he is trying to convey in the written medium.

80

The period or the comma always goes inside the closing quotation mark.

,"   ."

Examples:

1 The author announces at the beginning of his article that he is going to cite only "facts."

2 "I know," she said, "that you are telling me a barefaced lie."

3 Mrs. Robinson's "bearded, sandaled, unwashed hippies," many of whom had traveled over a thousand miles to the festival, represented an aggregation of straight-A students.

Mechanics

This is a clear case where usage, rather than logic, has established the prevailing convention. Many reputable British printers put the period or comma *outside* the closing quotation mark, especially when the quotation marks enclose something less than a complete sentence—e.g. a word or phrase or dependent clause. But American printers almost universally put the period or comma *inside* the closing quotation mark.

The advantage of such consistency is that you never have to pause and ask yourself, "Is this a case where the period goes inside or outside the quotation mark?" Whether it is a single word or a phrase or a dependent clause or an independent clause that is enclosed, the period or comma always goes *inside* the closing quotation mark.

In handwriting, take care to put the period or comma *inside* the quotation mark, not *under* it like this: ',' ',' In the case of quotations within quotations, both the single-stroke quotation mark and the double-stroke quotation go *outside* the period or the comma, as in this example:

"I read recently," he said, "that Patrick Henry never said, 'Give me liberty or give me death.'"

81

The colon or semicolon always goes outside the closing quotation mark.

"; ":

Examples:

1 He called this schedule of activities his "load": work, study, exercise, recreation, and sleep.

2 He told his taunters, ''I refuse to budge ''; his knees, however, were shaking even as he said those words.

Whereas the period or the comma always goes *inside* the closing quotation mark, the colon or the semicolon always goes *outside* it. If a writer has occasion to use quotation marks with a colon or a semicolon, he has only to recall that the convention governing the relationship of the colon or the semicolon to the closing quotation mark is just the opposite of the convention for the period and the comma.

82

The question mark sometimes goes inside, sometimes outside, the closing quotation mark.

$$?"\qquad\qquad "?$$

Examples:

1 Who was it that said, ''I regret that I have but one life to lose for my country ''?

2 He asked her bluntly, ''Will you marry me ?''

3 When will they stop asking, ''Who then is responsible for the war ?''

Although a period or a comma always goes inside the closing quotation mark and a colon or a semicolon always goes outside it, you have to consider each case individually before deciding whether to put the question mark inside or outside the closing quotation mark. Fortunately, the criteria for determining whether it goes inside or outside the quotation mark are fairly simple to apply:

Mechanics

(a) When the whole sentence, but not the unit enclosed in quotation marks, is a question, the question mark goes *outside* the closing quotation mark. (See the first example above.)

(b) When only the unit enclosed in quotation marks is a question, the question mark goes *inside* the closing quotation mark. (See the second example above.)

(c) When the whole sentence and the unit enclosed in quotation marks are both questions, the question mark goes *inside* the closing quotation mark. (See the third example above.)

In all cases, the question mark serves as the terminal punctuation for the entire sentence. In (*b*), you do not add a period outside the closing quotation mark, and in (*c*), you do not add another question mark outside the closing quotation mark.

83

The titles of books, newspapers, magazines, professional journals, plays, long poems, movies, radio programs, television programs, long musical compositions, works of art, and ships should be italicized by underlining.

Examples:

1 The critics have always rated Hemingway's *A Farewell to Arms* above his *For Whom the Bell Tolls.*

   (*titles of books*)

2 He has already published three articles in the *Quarterly Journal of Speech.*

   (*title of a professional journal*)

3 To support his contention, he quoted a passage from an anonymous article in *Newsweek*.

(*title of a magazine*)

4 The moonship *Falcon* settled down about 400 yards from the projected landing site.

(*title of the Apollo 15 "ship"*)

5 My parents insisted on watching *All in the Family*.

(*title of a television program*)

6 The critics unanimously panned the recent performance of *La Traviata*.

(*title of an opera*)

Printers use a special, italic, type, which slants slightly to the right, to set off certain words in a sentence from other words that are printed in regular roman type (upright letters). In handwriting or typewriting, one italicizes words by underlining them.

Although italics are used with the titles of all of the items listed above, the writer most often has occasion to use italics with the titles of book-length or pamphlet-length published materials. Besides being a convention, the use of italics for titles can also protect meaning in some instances. If someone wrote "I didn't really like Huckleberry Finn," a reader might be uncertain (unless the context gave him a clue) whether the writer was revealing his dislike for Mark Twain's novel or for the character of that name in the novel. If the writer intended to indicate that he disliked the novel, he could convey that message unambiguously by simply underlining (italicizing) the proper name.

How does one decide whether a poem is long enough to have its title italicized? As with most relative matters, the extreme cases are easily determinable. Obviously, a sonnet

Mechanics

would not qualify as a long poem, but Milton's *Paradise Lost* would. It is the middle-length poem that causes indecision. A reliable rule of thumb is this: if the poem was ever published as a separate book or if it could conceivably be published as a separate book, it could be considered long enough to be set forth in italics. According to that guideline, T. S. Eliot's *The Wasteland* would be considered a long poem, but his "The Love Song of J. Alfred Prufrock" would be considered a short poem and therefore should be enclosed in quotation marks (see **84**). But if you cannot decide whether a poem is "long" or "short," either italicize the title or enclose it in quotation marks and use that system consistently throughout the paper.

84

The titles of articles, essays, short stories, short poems, songs, and chapters of books should be enclosed in quotation marks.

Examples:

1 Thomas Gray's "Elegy Written in a Country Churchyard" is reputed to be the most anthologized poem in the English language.

(*title of a short poem*)

2 Hollis Alpert's "Movies Are Better Than the Stage" first appeared in the *Saturday Review of Literature.*

(*title of an article in a periodical*)

3 J. F. Powers's "The Valiant Woman" was reprinted in 1947 in *The Prince of Darkness and Other Stories.*

(*title of a short story in a collection of stories.*)

4 "Raindrops Keep Falling on My Head" set exactly the right mood for the bicycle caper in *Butch Cassidy and the Sundance Kid.*

(*title of a song*)

The general rule here is that the titles of published material that is *part* of a book or a periodical should be enclosed in quotation marks.

The title of a paper that you write should not be enclosed in quotation marks, nor should it be italicized. If your title contains elements that are normally italicized or enclosed in quotation marks, those elements, of course, should be italicized or enclosed in quotation marks.

The right and the wrong formats of a title for a paper submitted for a class assignment or for publication are illustrated here:

WRONG: "The Evolution of Courtly Love in Medieval Literature"

The Evolution of Courtly Love in Medieval Literature

RIGHT: The Evolution of Courtly Love in Medieval Literature

The Evolution of Courtly Love in Chaucer's Troilus and Criseyde

Courtly Love in Herrick's "Corinna's Going a-Maying" and Marvell's "To His Coy Mistress"

The Shift in Meaning of the Word Love in Renaissance Lyrics

"One Giant Step for Mankind"—Historic Words for a Historic Occasion

Mechanics

85

Italicize (underline) words referred to as words.

Examples of references to words as words:

1 He questioned the appropriateness of *honesty* in this context.
2 *The American Heritage Dictionary* defines *dudgeon* as "a sullen, angry, or indignant humor."
3 Unquestionably, *trudged* is a more specific verb than *walked*.
4 Look, for example, at his use of purely subjective words like *marvelous, exquisite,* and *wondrous.*

"He questioned the appropriateness of honesty in this context."

"He questioned the appropriateness of *honesty* in this context."

Although composed of the same words in the same order, those two sentences carry different meanings. The first sentence signifies that what is being challenged is the appropriateness of the thing (the abstract quality) designated by the word *honesty;* the second sentence signifies that what is being questioned is the appropriateness of the word itself. It is the italics alone that indicate to the reader the difference in meaning between these two sentences.

Italics (underlining) are a graphic device commonly used to distinguish a word being used *as a word* from that same word used as a symbol for an idea. (In handwritten or typewritten copy, you italicize words by underlining them.) An alternative but less common device for marking words used as words is to enclose the words in quotation marks, as in this example:

The heavy use of such sensory diction as "juicy," "empurpled," "smooth," "creaked," "murmuring" helps to evoke the scene and make it almost palpable to the reader.

Since both devices are authorized by convention, the writer should adopt one system and use it consistently. The use of italics is probably the safer of the two systems, however, because quotation marks are also used to enclose quoted words and phrases, as in the sentence, We heard her say "yes." (Here *yes* is not being referred to as a word but is a quotation of what she said.)

86

Italicize (underline) foreign words and phrases, unless they have become naturalized or Anglicized.

Examples of foreign words and phrases:

1 Why does the advertiser, whose mouthpiece is the copywriter, allow himself to be presented before the public as a poet *malgré lui*?
2 The advice to begin a short story as close to the climax as possible is a heritage of Horace's advice to begin a narrative *in medias res* rather than *ab ovo.*
3 There had been a remarkable revival in the late 1960s of the *Weltschmerz* that characterized the poetry of the Romantics.

So that the reader will not be even momentarily mystified by the sudden intrusion of strange-looking words into a stream of English words, printers use italics to underscore foreign words and phrases. The graphic device of italics does not ensure, of course, that the reader will be able to translate the foreign locution, but it does prevent confusion by alerting the reader to the presence of non-English words.

Some foreign words and phrases, like habeas corpus, divorcee, mania, siesta, subpoena, have been used so often in an English context that they have been accepted into the

Mechanics

vocabulary as "naturalized" English words and therefore as not needing to be set forth in italics. Dictionaries have a system for indicating which foreign words and phrases have become naturalized and which have *not* become naturalized. Since dictionaries sometimes differ in their judgments about the naturalized status of certain foreign expressions, the writer should consistently follow the dictates of the dictionary available to him in determining whether a word or phrase needs italics.

An obvious exception to the rule is that proper nouns designating foreign persons, places, and institutions, even when they retain their native spelling and pronunciation, are *always* set forth without italics (underlining).

87

Compound words should be hyphenated.

Examples of compound words:

1 Because I had the normal six-year-old's "sweet tooth," I was irresistibly lured by the candy store.

2 He was attracted to anti-Establishment movements because they lacked policy-making administrators.

3 They scheduled the examinations in three-quarter-hour segments.

4 He preferred eighteenth-century literature because of its urbanity.

5 A five- or six-story building should be all you will need for that kind of plant operation.

English reveals its Germanic origins in its tendency to form compounds—that is, to take two or more existent words and join them together to create a single unit that designates a thing or a concept quite different from what the individual words designate. A familiar example is the word **basketball.** When the two distinct words **basket** and **ball** were first joined to designate an athletic game or the kind of ball used in that game, the words were linked by a hyphen: **basket-ball.** When repeated use had made this new compound familiar to readers, the hyphen was dropped, and the two words were printed as a single word with no break between the two constituent parts.

Dozens of words in English have made this transition from a hyphenated compound to a single amalgamated word (e.g. *postoffice, skyscraper, briefcase, airport*). But hundreds of compounds are still printed with a hyphen, either because they have not been used enough to achieve status as un-marked hybrids or because the absence of a hyphen would lead to ambiguity. A reliable dictionary will indicate which compounds have made the passage and which have not.

With the exception of those words that have become recognized amalgams, a hyphen should be used to link

(a) two or more words functioning as a single grammatical unit.

his **never-say-die** attitude (adjective)
the junkyard had a huge **car-crusher** (noun)
the hoodlums **pistol-whipped** him (verb)
he conceded the point **willy-nilly** (adverb)

(b) two-word numbers (from 21 to 99) when they are written out.

twenty-one, thirty-six, forty-eight, ninety-nine

Mechanics

(c) combinations with prefixes **ex-** and **self-.**

ex-chairman, ex-wife, self-denial, self-contradictory

(d) combinations with prefixes like **anti-, pro-, pre-, post-,** when the second element in the combinations begins with a capital letter or a number.

anti-Establishment, pro-American, pre-1929, post-1945

(e) combinations with prefixes like **anti-, pro-, pre-, re-, semi-, sub-, over-,** when the second element begins with the letter that occurs at the end of the prefix.

anti-intellectual, pro-oxidant, pre-election, re-entry, semi-independent, sub-basement, over-refined

(f) combinations where the unhyphenated compound might be mistaken for another word.

re-cover (the chair)
recover (the lost wallet)
re-sign (the contract)
resign (his office)
co-op
coop

With these exceptions, compounds formed with these prefixes now tend to be written as a single word (e.g. *antiknock, preconscious, prodemocratic, postgraduate*). And at least one authority would have all the compounds in (*e*), above, spelled solid. As against this, other authorities make distinctions that allow for *preelection* and *reentry* while prohibiting *antiintellectual.* In adopting any system that makes such distinctions, the writer should consistently follow the conventions of the authority consulted.

Frequently in writing, only a hyphen will clarify ambiguous syntax. If the writer of the third sample sentence had not used

118

hyphens **(They scheduled the examinations in three quarter hour segments),** the reader would not be able to determine whether the examination was divided into three fifteen-minute segments (a meaning that would be clearly signaled by this placement of the hyphen: **three quarter-hour segments**) or whether it was divided into forty-five-minute segments (a meaning that is clearly signaled by this placement of hyphens: **three-quarter-hour segments**). There is a similar ambiguity in the sentence "He was the only new car dealer in town." A speaker would be able to clarify the ambiguous syntax of that sentence by the appropriate intonation of the voice. But in writing, only a hyphen will make clear whether the writer meant to say "He was the only new **car-dealer** in town" or "He was the only **new-car** dealer in town."

The fifth sample sentence shows how to hyphenate when there is more than one term on the left side of the hyphenation **(five-, six-).** In this way, **story** need not be repeated (as in · **A five-story or six-story building . . .**). In typing, a space is inserted after the hyphen if it does not immediately precede the word it is meant to join **(five- or;** NOT: **five-or).**

88

A word can be broken and hyphenated at the end of a line only at a syllable-break; a one-syllable word can never be broken and hyphenated.

For the writer, two valuable bits of information are supplied by the initial entry of every word in the dictionary: (1) the spelling of the word, and (2) the syllabification of the word. The word **belligerent,** for instance, is entered this way in the dictionary: **bel·lig·er·ent.** If that word occurred at the end of

Mechanics

a line and you saw that you could not get the whole word in the remaining space, you could break the word and hyphenate it at any of the syllables marked with a raised period. But you could not break the word in any of the following places: **bell-igerent, belli-gerent, bellige-rent.**

Since the syllabification of English words is often unpredictable, it is safest to consult a dictionary when you are in doubt about where syllable-breaks occur. But after a while, you learn certain "tricks" about syllabification that save you a trip to the dictionary. A word can usually be broken

(a) after a prefix **(con-, ad-, pre-, un-, im-).**

(b) before a suffix **(-tion, -ment, -less, -ous, -ing).**

(c) between double consonants **(oc-cur-rence, cop-per, prig-gish).**

One-syllable words, however, can never be divided and hyphenated, no matter how long they are. So if you come to the end of a line and find that you do not have enough space to squeeze in single-syllable words like *horde, grieve, stopped, quaint, strength, wrenched,* leave the space blank and write the whole word on the next line. You have no choice.

Even in the interest of preserving a right-hand margin, you should not divide a word so that only one or two letters of it stand at the end of the line or at the beginning of the next line. Faced with divisions like *a-bout, o-cean, un-healthy, grass-y, dioram-a, flor-id, smok-er, live-ly,* you should put the whole word on that line or the next one. Remember that the hyphen itself takes up one space.

89

Observe the conventions governing the use of numbers in written copy.

Examples of violations of the conventions:

1 **522** men reported to the recruiting center.
2 During the first half of the **20th** century, **28 4**-year colleges and **14 2**-year colleges adopted collective-bargaining agencies.
3 The cocktail party started at **four P.M. in the afternoon.**
4 An account of the Wall Street crash of October **twenty-ninth, nineteen hundred and twenty-nine** begins on page **fifty-five.**
5 About **six and a half %** of the stores were selling a gross of **three-by-five** index cards for more than **thirty-six dollars and thirty-eight cents.**

The most common conventions governing the use of numbers in written copy are as follows:

(a) Do not begin a sentence with an Arabic number; spell out the number or recast the sentence:

Five hundred and twenty-two men reported to the recruiting center.
OR: A total of **522** men reported to the recruiting center.

(b) Spell out any number of less than three digits (or any number under 101) when the number is used as an adjective modifying a noun:

During the first half of the **twentieth** century, **twenty-eight four-**year colleges and **fourteen two-**year colleges adopted collective-bargaining agencies.

(c) Always use Arabic numbers with A.M. and P.M. and do not add the redundant **o'clock** and **morning** or **afternoon:**

Mechanics

The cocktail party started at **4:00** P.M.
OR: The cocktail party started at **four o'clock in the afternoon.**

(d) Use Arabic numbers for dates and page numbers:

An account of the Wall Street crash of October **29, 1919** begins on page **55.**

(e) Use Arabic numbers for addresses (618 N. 29th St.), dollars and cents ($4.68, $0.15 or 15 cents), decimals (3.14, 0.475), degrees (52°F.), measurements (especially when abbreviations are used: 3" × 5", 3.75 mi., 2 ft. 9 in., 6'2" tall, but *six feet tall*), percentages (6% or 6 percent, but always use **percent** with fractional percentages—$6\frac{1}{2}$ percent or 6.5 percent):

About **$6\frac{1}{2}$ percent** of the stores were selling a gross of **3" × 5"** index cards for more than **$36.38.**

90

Observe the conventions governing the capitalization of certain words.

Examples:

1 **P**resident **G**erald **R**. **F**ord informed the members of **C**ongress that he was appointing **M**s. **S**hirley **T**emple **B**lack as the **U**nited **S**tates ambassador to **G**hana.

2 **T**he title of the article in the *New Yorker* was "**T**he **T**ime of **I**llusion."

3 **D**r. **T**homas **J**. **C**ade, a professor in the **D**ivision of **B**iological **S**ciences at **C**ornell **U**niversity, has been supervising the breeding of peregrines captured in the **A**rctic, the **W**est, and the **P**acific **N**orthwest.

4 **T**he prime vacation time for most **A**mericans is the period between the **F**ourth of **J**uly and **L**abor **D**ay.

90 Capitalization, of Certain Words

5 The Korean troops resisted the incursion of the Communist forces.

In general, the convention governing capitalization is that the first letter of the proper name (that is, the particular or exclusive name) of persons, places, things, institutions, agencies, etc., should be capitalized. While the tendency today is to use lowercase letters for many words that formerly were written or printed with capital letters (for instance, *biblical reference* instead of **B**iblical *reference*), the use of capital letters still prevails in the following cases:

(a) The first letter of the first word of a sentence.

They were uncertain about which words should be capitalized.

(b) The first letter of the first word of every line of English verse.

Little fly,
Thy summer's play
My thoughtless hand
Has brushed away.

(c) All nouns, pronouns, verbs, adjectives, adverbs, and first and last words of titles of publications and other artistic works.

Remembrance of Things Past (see **83**)
"The Place of the Enthymeme in Rhetorical Theory" (see **84**)
"A Tent That Families Can Live In"
The Return of the Pink Panther

(d) The first name, middle name or initial, and last name of a person, real or fictional.

H.R. Haldeman   Sylvia Marie Mikkelsen
David Copperfield   Achilles

Mechanics

(e) The names and abbreviations of villages, towns, cities, counties, states, nations, and regions.

Chillicothe, Ohio   Franklin County
U.S.A.   Soviet Union
Indo-China   Arctic Circle
the Western World   South America
the Midwestern states   the South (but: we drove
            south)

(f) The names of rivers, lakes, falls, oceans, mountains, deserts, parks.

the Mississippi River   Atlantic
the Grand Tetons   Yellowstone National Park
Lake Erie   Victoria Falls

(g) The names and abbreviations of businesses, industries, institutions, agencies, schools, political parties, religious denominations, and philosophical, literary, and artistic movements.

University of Nebraska   Democrats
the Republican convention   C.I.A.
Dow Chemical Corporation   John Wiley & Sons, Publishers
Communist(s) (but: a com-   Smithsonian Institution
munist ideology)   Japan Air Lines
Victorian literature   the Pentagon
Thomistic philosophy   Pure Land Buddhism

(h) The titles of historical events, epochs, and periods.

Renaissance   Thirty Years' War
World War II   Ice Age
the Middle Ages   the Battle of Gettysburg
Reformation   the Depression

(i) Honorary and official titles when they precede the name of the person and when they are used in place of the name of a specific person.

90 Capitalization, of Certain Words

former **P**resident **E**isen-
hower
the **D**uke of **C**ornwall
Pope **P**aul
His (**H**er) **E**xcellency

Senator **E**dward **K**ennedy
General **P**atton
the **C**hief **J**ustice
Queen **E**lizabeth
Sri **R**amakrishna

(j) The names of weekdays, months, holidays, holy days, and other special days or periods.

Christmas **E**ve
Passover
Lent
Mardi **G**ras

Memorial **D**ay
the **F**ourth of **J**uly
National **B**ook **W**eek
the first **S**unday in **J**une

(k) The names and abbreviations of the books and divisions of the Bible and other sacred books (no italics for these titles).

Genesis
Matt. (**G**ospel of **M**atthew)
Epistle to the Romans
King **J**ames **V**ersion
Talmud
Book of **J**ob
Pss. (**P**salms)

Pentateuch
Acts of the **A**postles
Vulgate
Koran
Scriptures
Bhagavad **G**ita
Lotus **S**utra

Exceptions: Do not capitalize words like the underlined in the following examples:

the African coast (but: the
West Coast)
northern Wisconsin
the senator from Wyoming
the municipal library

the river Elbe (but: the Elbe
River)
the federal government
the presidential itinerary
the county courthouse

Format of the Research Paper

General Instructions

A research paper reports the results of some investigation, experiment, interview, or reading that you have done. Some of the ordinary papers you write are also based on personal investigations, interviews, and reading, and when they are based on external sources, you should acknowledge those sources in the text of your paper. For instance, you can reveal the source of information or quotations by saying in the text "Mr. Stanley Smith, the director of the Upward Bound project, with whom I talked last week, confirmed the rumor that . . ." or "James Reston said in his column in last Sunday's *New York Times* that . . ." Authors of research papers also use identifying lead-ins like those in the text, but in addition they supply, in footnotes, any further bibliographical information (for instance, the exact date of the newspaper you are quoting from and the number of the page on which the passage occurred) that readers would need if they wanted to check the sources. By revealing this specific information about the source, the author enables his readers to check whether he has been accurate or fair in his reporting, and he also enhances his credibility.

In the pages that follow, we will present some advice about gathering and reporting material from outside sources, some models for footnote and bibliography forms, and a sample research paper. The instructor or the journal that you write for may prescribe a format that differs from the advice given here, but if no specific instructions are given, you can follow these suggestions and models with the assurance that they conform to the prevailing conventions for research papers.

(A) GATHERING NOTES

Each person eventually discovers a system of gathering notes that works best for him. Some people, for instance, just scribble their notes on full sheets of paper or in spiral note-books. The system that works best for most researchers, however, is to record notes and quotations on 3 x 5 or 4 x 6 cards—*one* note or quotation to a card. The advantage of having your notes on cards is that later you can select and arrange the cards to suit the order in which you are going to use them in your paper. It is considerably more difficult to select and arrange notes if they are written out, one after the other, on full sheets of paper.

(B) SELF-CONTAINED NOTECARDS

Each notecard should be self-contained—that is, it should contain all the information you would need to document that material properly if you used it in your paper. A notecard is self-contained if you never have to go back to the original source to recover any bit of information about the note. So each notecard should carry at least this much information:

1 The card should carry some indication whether the note is paraphrased or quoted verbatim. Don't trust your memory to be able to distinguish later whether a note is paraphrased or quoted.

Format of the Research Paper

2 If quoted material covers more than one page in the source from which it was copied, you should devise some system of indicating just where the quoted material went over to the next page. If later you use only part of that quotation, you have to know whether to cite one page (p. 189) or two pages (pp. 189–90) in the footnote. Some notation like (→ p. 190) inserted in the notecard after the last word on the page (in this case, after the last word on p. 189) in the original source will help you determine later whether you need to cite one page or two pages.

3 The notecard should contain all the bibliographical information needed to document the note in a footnote of your paper: name of the author, title of the book or article, publication information, and page numbers (see Model Footnotes). If you are taking several notes from the same source, you can devise some shorthand system so that you do not have to write out all the bibliographical information on every notecard.

(C) WHAT NEEDS TO BE FOOTNOTED?

You will have to develop a sense for what needs to be documented with a footnote. Here are some guidelines to help you:

1 Ordinarily, every direct quotation should carry a footnote. However, if you were doing a research paper on, say, a novel, you could be spared having to document every quotation from the novel by using a footnote like this the *first time* you quote from the novel:

> [8]John Steinbeck, The Grapes of Wrath (New York: Viking Press, 1939), p. 134. Hereafter all quotations from this first edition of the novel will be documented with a page number in parentheses immediately after the quotation.

Format of the Research Paper

2 Paraphrased material may or may not need a footnote. If the fact or information that you report in your own words is *generally known* by people knowledgeable on the subject, you probably would not have to document that paraphrased material. For instance, if you were writing a research paper on the assassination of Abraham Lincoln, you probably would not have to document your statement that John Wilkes Booth shot Lincoln in Ford's Theater in Washington in April of 1865, because that historical fact is common knowledge. But if one of the arguments in your paper concerned the *exact time of the day* when he was shot, you would have to document your statement that Lincoln was shot at 8:40 P.M. on the evening of April 14, 1865. When, however, you cannot resolve your doubt about whether paraphrased material needs to be documented with a footnote that reveals the source of the information, document it.

3 When you are summarizing, in your own words, a great deal of information that you have gathered from your reading, you can be spared having to document several sentences in that summary by putting a footnote number after the *first sentence* of the summary and using a footnote like this:

> [10]For the biographical information presented in this and the subsequent paragraph, I am indebted to Minnie M. Brashear, Mark Twain: Son of Missouri (Chapel Hill: University of North Carolina Press, 1934), pp. 34–65 and Gamaliel Bradford, "Mark Twain," Atlantic Monthly, 125 (April, 1920), 462–73.

(D) KEEP QUOTATIONS TO A MINIMUM

A research paper should not be just a pastiche of long quotations stitched together by an occasional comment or by a transitional sentence by the author of the paper. You should

Format of the Research Paper

use your own words as much as possible, and when you do quote, you should keep the quotation brief. Often a quoted phrase or sentence will make a point more emphatically than a long quotation. You must learn to look for the phrase or sentence that represents the kernel of the quotation and to use that extract rather than the full quotation. Otherwise, the point you want to make with the quotation may be lost in all the verbiage. You will be more likely to keep your quotations short if you try to work most of the quotations into the framework of your own sentence, like this:

> Frank Ellis calls such an interpretation "the biographical fallacy, the assumption that an exact, one-to-one correspondence exists between the person who is imagined to be speaking the lines of the poem (the Spokesman) and the historical personage who is known to have written the poem."[12]

Sometimes, however, when you find it difficult to present the essential point in a short extract, you will have to quote something at greater length. Long quotations (two sentences or more) should be *inset* from the left-hand margin and *single-spaced,* with *no quotation marks enclosing the quotation,* like this:

> Frank Ellis offers this cogent argument to refute the charge that the Epitaph is not integrated with the rest of the poem:

> The evidence for this is said to lie in the
> fact that there are disparities between the
> two accounts that are given of the Stonecut-
> ter, one by the aged Swain and the other in
> Epitaph. But it has never been pointed out
> that these disparities are deliberate and
> dramatic. The illiterate old rustic is un-
> sympathetic. His disapproval has been soft-
> ened no doubt by death, but it is still ap-
> parent that to him the Stonecutter seemed
> lazy, queer, unsociable, and probably crazy.
> But the Epitaph enables the reader to see
> around this characterization. For the
> Spokesman, who composed the Epitaph, is an
> outlander, a fellow poeta ignotus, and
> therefore unsympathetic.[15]

(E) USE A LEAD-IN FOR ALL QUOTATIONS

Every direct quotation should be accompanied by a lead-in phrase or clause, which at least identifies by name the person who is about to speak. But it further aids coherence if the lead-in also points up the pertinence of the subsequent quotation to what you have been talking about or to what you are going to talk about. Here are some typical identifying and orienting lead-ins:

> Edmund Wilson countered this charge by saying
> that "there is never any reason for supposing
> that anybody but the governess sees the
> ghosts."

Format of the Research Paper

"It apparently did not occur to any of Wilson's critics," says Oscar Cargill in defense of Wilson's interpretation, "that James might have an adequate motive for disguising his purpose in the tale."

Robert Heilman has this to say about Wilson's interpretation of Henry James's haunting story:

(following this last lead-in would be either a single sentence enclosed in quotation marks or a series of sentences inset and single-spaced, like the extended quotation in [D] *above)*

(F) THE FORMAT OF FOOTNOTES

The first line of every footnote is indented from the left-hand margin (usually the same number of spaces as paragraph indentations in the body of the paper), but any subsequent lines of the same footnote are brought out to the left-hand margin. If footnotes are put at the bottom of the page, they are single-spaced *within* the footnote and double-spaced *between* footnotes. If footnotes are put on separate pages, they are double-spaced both *within* the footnote and *between* footnotes. See Model Footnotes and the Sample Research Paper for further information about the format of footnotes.

(G) PRIMARY AND SECONDARY FOOTNOTES

Primary footnote forms (that is, those giving full bibliographical information) must be used the *first time* a source is cited. Thereafter, that same source can be documented with a secondary footnote form (that is, a shortened form). See Model Footnotes and the Sample Research Paper for the format of primary and secondary footnotes.

(H) THE FORMAT OF BIBLIOGRAPHICAL ENTRIES

Bibliographical entries are arranged alphabetically on separate pages at the end of the research paper. The list of entries is alphabetized according to the last name of the author (or, in the case of unsigned articles, according to the first significant word in the title). For that reason, the names of authors are inverted in the bibliography—e.g. **Heilman, Robert.** The first line of each bibliographical entry begins at the left-hand margin, and any subsequent lines in that entry are indented (just the opposite of the format of footnotes). Bibliographical entries are single-spaced *within* the entry and double-spaced *between* entries. (If, however, the paper is being submitted for publication, the bibliographical entries are double-spaced both within the entry and between entries.) See models for Bibliography (p. 145) for other differences between the format of footnotes and the format of bibliographical entries.

(I) ELLIPSIS PERIODS

Ellipsis periods (three spaced periods) are used to indicate that words or whole sentences have been omitted from a direct quotation:

Format of the Research Paper

> The President said last week that "the Ameri-
> can people . . . would not tolerate such vio-
> lence."

(note that there is a space between periods; wrong form: ...)

> Philip Gove said in a letter to the <u>New York Times</u>:
>
> > The paragraph is, of course, a monstrosity,
> > totally removed from possible occurrence in
> > connection with any genuine attempt to use
> > words in normally expected context. . . . A
> > similar artificial monstrosity could be con-
> > trived by jumbling together inappropriate
> > words from formal literary language or from
> > the Second Edition.

(the fourth period in this instance is the period used to mark the end of the sentence. Because of this period and the capital letter with which the next group of words begins, we know that at least the end of the first sentence has been omitted and that possibly as much as a whole paragraph has been removed before the next sentence)

Usually there is no need to put ellipsis periods at the beginning or end of a quotation, because the reader knows that the quotation has been extracted from a larger context. Reserve ellipsis periods for indicating omissions *within* quotations.

Format of the Research Paper

(J) SQUARE BRACKETS

Square brackets are used to enclose anything that the author of the research paper inserts into a direct quotation from another author:

> About this tendency to indulge in scatological language, H. A. Taine wrote, "He [Swift] drags poetry not only through the mud, but into the filth; he rolls in it like a raging madman, he enthrones himself in it, and bespatters all passers-by."

> The Senator was emphatic in stating his reaction to the measure: "This action by HEW [Health, Education, and Welfare] will definitely not reverse the downward spiral [of prices and wages] that has plagued us for the last eight months."

> We find this entry in the Japanese admiral's diary: "Promptly at 8:32 on Sunday morning of December 6 [sic], 1941, I dispatched the first wave of bombers for the raid on Perl Harber [sic]."

Format of the Research Paper

(**sic** *is a Latin adverb meaning "thus," "in this manner," and is used to let the reader know that the error in logic or fact or grammar or spelling in the quotation has been copied exactly as it was in the original source. It is italicized because it is a foreign word*)

If your typewriter does not have keys that make square brackets, you will have to draw the brackets with a pen after you remove the paper from the typewriter.

Format of the Research Paper:
Model Footnotes

The models for footnotes and for bibliography follow the forms prescribed in *The MLA Style Sheet,* 2nd ed. (New York: Modern Language Association, 1970), one of the most widely used systems in America.

The models here are single-spaced within the footnote and double-spaced between footnotes, as they would be if they appeared at the bottom of the page in a research paper or a dissertation. For the double-spacing of footnotes, see the Model for Footnotes Entered on Separate Pages on p. 167.

For the bibliography form for each of these model footnotes, see the next section (p. 147).

(K) PRIMARY FOOTNOTES

(the first reference to a source)

(1) A single book by a single author:

[14]Hozen Seki, <u>The Great Natural Way</u> (New York: American Buddhist Academy, 1976), p. 88.

Format of the Research Paper

> 8John W. Landon, <u>Jesse</u> <u>Crawford</u>: <u>Poet</u> <u>of</u> <u>the</u>
> <u>Organ</u>, <u>Wizard</u> <u>of</u> <u>the</u> <u>Mighty</u> <u>Wurlitzer</u> (Vestal,
> N.Y.: The Vestal Press, 1974), pp. 75-6.

(*Notice that the first line of the footnote is indented and that subsequent lines of the footnote start at the left-hand margin. The **p.** is the abbreviation of **page; pp.** is the abbreviation of **pages.**)*

(2) A single book by more than one author:

> 12Paul A. Baran and Paul M. Sweezy, <u>Monop-</u>
> <u>oly</u> <u>Capital</u> (New York: Monthly Review Press,
> 1966), p. 392.

(3) A book of more than one volume:

> 13William Lee Hays and Robert L. Winkler,
> <u>Statistics</u>: <u>Probability</u>, <u>Inference</u>, <u>and</u> <u>Deci-</u>
> <u>sion</u> (New York: Holt, Rinehart, and Winston,
> 1970), II, 137.

(*Whenever a volume number is cited [here the Roman numeral **II**], the abbreviation **p.** or **pp.** is not used in front of the page number.*)

(4) A book edited by one or more editors:

> 3<u>Essays</u> <u>in</u> <u>American</u> <u>Economic</u> <u>History</u>, ed.
> Alfred W. Coats and Ross M. Robertson (London:
> Edward Arnold, 1969), pp. 268-9.

> [9]The Letters of Jonathan Swift to Charles
> Ford, ed. David Nichol Smith (Oxford: Clarendon
> Press, 1935), p. 187.

*(Here the abbreviation **ed.** stands for **edited by.**)*

(5) An essay or a chapter by an author in an edited collection:

> [2]Martin J. Svaglic, "Classical Rhetoric and
> Victorian Prose," The Art of Victorian Prose,
> ed. George Levine and William Madden (New
> York: Oxford Univ. Press, 1968), pp. 268–70.

(6) A new edition of a book:

> [5]Oswald Doughty, A Victorian Romantic,
> Dante Gabriel Rossetti, 2nd ed. (London: Ox-
> ford Univ. Press, 1960), p. 35.

*(Here the abbreviation **ed.** stands for **edition.**)*

(7) A book that is part of a series:

> [26]William Heytesbury, Medieval Logic and
> the Rise of Mathematical Physics. University
> of Wisconsin Publications in Medieval Science,
> No. 3 (Madison: Univ. of Wisconsin Press, 1956),
> p. 97.

*(Here the abbreviation **No.** stands for **Number.**)*

Format of the Research Paper

(8) A book in a paperback series:

> [11]Edmund Wilson, <u>To</u> <u>the</u> <u>Finland</u> <u>Station</u>.
> Anchor Books (Garden City, N.Y.: Doubleday,
> 1955), p. 130.

(9) A translation:

> [6]Fyodor Dostoevsky, <u>Crime</u> <u>and</u> <u>Punishment</u>,
> trans. Constance Garnett (New York: Heritage
> Press, 1938), p. 351.
>
> [7]Jacques Ellul, <u>A</u> <u>Critique</u> <u>of</u> <u>the</u> <u>New</u> <u>Com-</u>
> <u>monplaces</u>, trans. Helen Weaver (New York:
> Knopf, 1968), pp. 139–40.

*(The abbreviation **trans.** stands for **translated by.**)*

(10) A signed and an unsigned article from an encyclopedia:

> [4]J. A. Ewing, "Steam-Engine and Other Heat-
> Engines," <u>Encyclopaedia</u> <u>Britannica</u>, 9th ed.
> XXII, 475–7.
>
> [10]"Dwarfed Trees," <u>Encyclopaedia</u> <u>Americana</u>,
> 1948, IX, 445.

*(Since encyclopedias periodically undergo revision and
updating, the particular edition consulted should be indicated by a date or a number. In the bibliography, unsigned
articles are filed alphabetically according to the first sig-*

nificant word in the title—here Dwarfed.)

(11) An article from a journal:

> [12]Nelson Adkins, "Emerson and the Bardic Tradition," <u>PMLA</u>, 72 (1948), 665.
>
> [8]Theodore Otto Windt, Jr., "The Diatribe: Last Resort for Protest," <u>QJS</u>, 58 (1972), 9–10.

(*Well-known scholarly journals are commonly referred to by their abbreviated titles. Here* PMLA *stands for* Publications of the Modern Language Association; QJS *stands for* Quarterly Journal of Speech. *Volume numbers of journals are now designated by an Arabic number [here 72 and 58] rather than, as formerly, by a Roman numeral. Because the volume number has been cited, the abbreviations p. and pp. are not used in front of the page numbers.*)

(12) An article in a popular magazine:

> [4]Robert J. Levin, "Sex, Morality, and Society," <u>Saturday Review</u>, 9 July 1966, p. 29.
>
> [7]Charles E. Silberman, "Technology Is Knocking on the Schoolhouse Door," <u>Fortune</u>, Aug. 1966, pp. 121–2.

(*Note that* Saturday Review *is a weekly magazine;* Fortune *is a monthly. Because no volume number is cited, p. and pp. are used in front of the page numbers.*)

Format of the Research Paper

(13) A signed and an unsigned article in a newspaper:

> [15]Art Gilman, "Altering U.S. Flag for Political Causes Stirs a Legal Debate," _Wall Street Journal_, 12 June 1970, p. 1.
>
> [26]"Twin Games Bid: Wrestling, Judo," _New York Times_, 9 April 1972, Section 5, p. 15, cols. 4-6.

(For editions of a newspaper with multiple sections, each with its own pagination, it is necessary to cite the section in addition to the page number. It is helpful also to give column numbers. Sometimes, if an article appeared in one edition of a newspaper but not in other editions, it is necessary to specify the particular edition of the newspaper—e.g. New York Times, _Late City Ed., 4 Feb. 1972, p. 12, col. 1.)_

(14) A signed book review:

> [19]John F. Dalbor, rev. of _Meaning and Mind: A Study in the Psychology of Language_, by Robert F. Terwilliger, _Philosophy & Rhetoric_, 5 (1972), 60-1.
>
> [3]Brendan Gill, rev. of _Ibsen_, by Michael Meyer, _New Yorker_, 8 April 1972, p. 128.

(The first review appeared in a scholarly journal; the second review appeared in a weekly magazine. The abbreviation **rev.** stands for **review.**)

142

(L) SECONDARY FOOTNOTES

(shortened forms after a source has once been given in full)

15Seki, p. 80.

(*This is the shortened form of the first footnote given in (1) under* Primary Footnotes.)

16Hays and Winkler, II, 140.

(*This is the shortened form of the footnote given in (3) under* Primary Footnotes.)

17Ibid., I, 87.

(***Ibid.*** *is the abbreviation of the Latin adverb* ***ibidem,*** *meaning "in the same place." Ibid. may be used if the source in that footnote is the same as the one cited in the immediately preceding footnote. However, if a reader would have to turn back one or more pages to find the last source cited, it would be better to use the last-name shortened form: Hays and Winkler, I, 87. There must be added to Ibid. only what changes from the previous source. Thus in footnote 17 above, 1 and 87 were added to Ibid., because both the volume number and the page number changed from the previous footnote. If only the page number changed, footnote 17 would read thus: Ibid., p. 145. If nothing changed, footnote 17 would read thus: Ibid.)*

18Wilson, Finland Station, pp. 220-2.

Format of the Research Paper

(*When more than one book or article by the same author has been cited in a paper, you must use an abbreviated title in addition to the surname of the author in order to identify the source. In footnote 18 above,* Finland Station *is an abbreviated form of the full title* To the Finland Station.)

```
19"Rendezvous with Ecology," p. 97.
```

(*In the case of an anonymous article or book, the title or a shortened form of it has to be used in subsequent references to that source.*)

(M)
Format of the Research Paper:
Models for Bibliography

The form of a bibliography entry differs in some ways from that of a footnote reference. The following shows how the two forms handle a citation for the same book.

BIBLIOGRAPHY

```
Ryan, Edwin. A Col-
   lege Handbook to
   Newman. Washing-
   ton, D.C.: Catho-
   lic Education
   Press, 1930.
```

The first line begins at the left-hand margin, with all subsequent lines indented.

FOOTNOTE

```
    8Edwin Ryan, A
College Handbook to
Newman (Washington,
D.C.: Catholic Edu-
cation Press, 1930),
p. 109.
```

The first line is indented, with all subsequent lines brought out to the left-hand margin.

Format of the Research Paper

BIBLIOGRAPHY	FOOTNOTE
The name of the author is inverted (last name first) for purposes of alphabetizing the list of entries.	The name of the author is set down in the normal order.
The three main divisions of author, title, and publishing data are separated by periods.	The three main divisions of author, title, and publishing data are separated by commas.
Place of publication, name of the publisher, and publication date follow the title, without parentheses.	Place of publication, name of the publisher, and publication date are enclosed in parentheses.
The subtitle, if any, should be included in the citation. See (2) below.	The subtitle, if any, may be omitted in the citation.
There is no page reference unless the entry is for an article or part of a collection, in which case the full span of pages (first page and last page) is cited.	Only a specific page reference is cited.

CORRESPONDING BIBLIOGRAPHY FORMS FOR THE FOURTEEN MODEL FOOTNOTES

(If the research paper is submitted as an assignment in a

course, the bibliography entries may be single-spaced within the entry and double-spaced between entries, as in the Model for a Bibliography Page (p. 165). If, however, the paper is being submitted to a journal for possible publication, the entries should be double-spaced both within the entry and between the entries, as they are in these models.)

(1) A single book by a single author:

```
Seki, Hozen. The Great Natural Way. New York:
    American Buddhist Academy, 1976.
Landon, John W. Jesse Crawford: Poet of the
    Organ, Wizard of the Mighty Wurlitzer. Ves-
    tal, N.Y.: The Vestal Press, 1974.
```

(2) A single book by more than one author:

```
Baran, Paul A., and Paul M. Sweezy. Monopoly
    Capital: An Essay on American Economic and
    Social Order. New York: Monthly Review
    Press, 1966.
```

(Only the name of the first author should be inverted. Notice that the subtitle, which was omitted in the footnote, is included here.)

(3) A book of more than one volume:

Format of the Research Paper

Hays, William Lee, and Robert L. Winkler. <u>Sta-</u>
<u>tistics</u>: <u>Probability</u>, <u>Inference</u>, <u>and</u> <u>Deci-</u>
    <u>sion</u>. 2 vols. New York: Holt, Rinehart, and
    Winston, 1970.

(4) A book edited by one or more editors:

<u>Essays</u> <u>in</u> <u>American</u> <u>Economic</u> <u>History</u>. Ed.
    Alfred W. Coats and Ross M. Robertson. Lon-
    don: Edward Arnold, 1969.
<u>The</u> <u>Letters</u> <u>of</u> <u>Jonathan</u> <u>Swift</u> <u>to</u> <u>Charles</u> <u>Ford</u>.
    Ed. David Nichol Smith. Oxford: Clarendon
    Press, 1935.

(In the bibliography, these books would be filed alphabetically according to the first significant word in the
title—**Essays** and **Letters** respectively.)

(5) An essay or a chapter by an author in an
    edited collection:

Svaglic, Martin J. "Classical Rhetoric and Vic-
    torian Prose." <u>The</u> <u>Art</u> <u>of</u> <u>Victorian</u> <u>Prose</u>.
    Ed. George Levine and William Madden. New
    York: Oxford Univ. Press, 1968, pp. 268-88.

148

(Because this essay is part of a collection, the full span of pages is cited in the bibliography.)

(6) A new edition of a book:

```
Doughty, Oswald. A Victorian Romantic, Dante
     Gabriel Rossetti. 2nd ed. London: Oxford
     Univ. Press, 1960.
```

(7) A book that is part of a series:

```
Heytesbury, William. Medieval Logic and the
     Rise of Mathematical Physics. University of
     Wisconsin Publications in Medieval Science,
     No. 3. Madison: Univ. of Wisconsin Press,
     1956.
```

(8) A book in a paperback series:

```
Wilson, Edmund. To the Finland Station. Anchor
     Books. Garden City, N.Y.: Doubleday, 1955.
```

(9) A translation:

```
Dostoevsky, Fyodor. Crime and Punishment.
     Trans. Constance Garnett. New York: Herit-
     age Press, 1938.
```

Format of the Research Paper

```
Ellul, Jacques. A Critique of the New Common-
     places. Trans. Helen Weaver. New York:
     Knopf, 1968.
```

(10) A signed and an unsigned article from an encyclopedia:

```
Ewing, J. A. "Steam-Engine and Other Heat-
     Engines." Encyclopaedia Britannica. 9th ed.,
     XXII, 473-526.
"Dwarfed Trees." Encyclopaedia Americana. 1948,
     IX, 445-6.
```

(Notice that the full span of pages of these articles is given.)

(11) An article from a journal:

```
Adkins, Nelson. "Emerson and the Bardic Tradi-
     tion." Publications of the Modern Language
     Association, 72 (1948), 662-7.
Windt, Theodore Otto, Jr. "The Diatribe: Last
     Resort for Protest." Quarterly Journal of
     Speech, 58 (1972), 1-14.
```

(Although in footnotes well-known scholarly journals are commonly referred to by their abbreviated title, it is advisable to give the full title in the bibliography.)

Format of the Research Paper

(12) An article in a popular magazine:

Levin, Robert J. "Sex, Morality, and Society."

    Saturday Review, 9 July 1966, pp. 29-30.

Silberman, Charles E. "Technology Is Knocking

    on the Schoolhouse Door." _Fortune_, Aug.

    1966, pp. 120-25.

(13) A signed and an unsigned article in a newspaper:

Gilman, Art. "Altering U. S. Flag for Political

    Causes Stirs a Legal Debate." _Wall Street Jour-_

    nal, 12 June 1970, p. 1.

"Twin Games Bid: Wrestling, Judo." _New York Times_,

    9 April 1972, Section 5, p. 15, cols. 4-6.

(14) A signed book review:

Dalbor, John B. Review of _Meaning and Mind: A_

    Study in the Psychology of Language, by

    Robert F. Terwilliger. _Philosophy & Rheto-_

    ric, 5 (1972), 60-61.

Gill, Brendan. Review of _Ibsen_, by Michael

    Meyer. _New Yorker_, 8 April 1972, pp. 126-

    30.

**Format of the Research Paper: Model Research Paper
(with footnotes at bottom of page)**

A Study of the Various Interpretations
of
"Young Goodman Brown"

Diana Lynn Ikenberry
English 302
January 7, 1977

A Study of the Various Interpretations
of
"Young Goodman Brown"

Nathaniel Hawthorne's "Young Goodman Brown" has been
subjected to various interpretations. A prime reason for so
many different interpretations is the story's extremely ambiguous nature. One critic seldom agrees with another as to
why various parts of the story are ambiguous. One question
that has engaged many critics is whether Goodman Brown actually went into the forest and met the devil or whether he
only dreamed that he did. Richard Fogle is one critic who
believes that Hawthorne failed to answer this question defin-
itively, because "the ambiguities of meaning are intentional,
an integral part of his purpose."[1] Fogle feels that the
ambiguity results from unanswered questions like the one
above. And it is just this ambiguity or "device of multiple
choice,"[2] as Fogle calls it, that is the very essence of
"Young Goodman Brown."

Critic Thomas F. Walsh, Jr. went a step further in
analyzing the ambiguity of Brown's journey into the forest.[3]
He agreed with Fogle that the reader can never be certain
whether the journey was real or imaginary; however, the

---

[1] Richard H. Fogle, "Ambiguity and Clarity in Hawthorne's
'Young Goodman Brown,'" New England Quarterly, 18 (December,
1945), 448.

[2] Ibid., p. 449.

[3] Thomas F. Walsh, Jr., "The Bedeviling of Young Goodman
Brown," Modern Language Quarterly, 19 (December, 1958), 331-6.

Format of the Research Paper

reader can be certain "not only of the nature and stages of Goodman Brown's despair, but also of its probable cause."[4] Walsh also points out that the effect upon Brown, once he emerges from the forest, is quite clear: "Goodman Brown lived and died an unhappy, despairing man."[5] It is Walsh's view that the only solution to the problem of ambiguity in relation to what happened in the forest can be found in the story's complex symbolic pattern.

D. M. McKeithan's view of Brown's journey is unlike any of the previously mentioned views. He feels that, in reality, Goodman Brown neither journeyed into the forest that night nor dreamed that he did. What Brown did do, according to McKeithan, was "to indulge in sin (represented by the journey into the forest that night . . .)," thinking that he could break away from his sinfulness whenever he chose to.[6] However, Brown indulged in sin longer than he expected and "suffered the consequences, which were the loss of religious faith and faith in all other human beings."[7]

All of these critics have something to add to readers' notions about the ambiguous nature of "Young Goodman Brown." It is the purpose of this paper to study some of these critics' interpretations, as well as the interpretations of some critics

---

[4] Ibid., p. 332.

[5] Walsh, p. 336.

[6] D. M. McKeithan, "Hawthorne's 'Young Goodman Brown': An Interpretation," <u>Modern Language Notes</u>, 67 (February, 1952), 96.

[7] Ibid.

Model Research Paper

not yet mentioned, to see just exactly what they have to add
to the interpretation of Hawthorne's masterpiece. I will focus primarily on two areas of interpretations: the realizations of Goodman Brown's faith and the over-all implications
of the story itself. These two areas proved to be quite
controversial.

Despite all the ambiguities of meaning mentioned above,
I must conclude that young Goodman Brown did come to some
realizations about his own personal faith. When Brown starts
out on his journey into the forest, he is confident that his
faith will carry him to heaven. As Thomas E. Connolly points
out, "it is in this concept that his disillusionment will
come."[8] I must agree with Connolly's statement, for Brown
thinks that his wife delayed his journey, but when he ar-
rives at the meeting place with the devil, his Faith is already there. Brown's confidence in his virtuous wife has
been shattered, and from this point on, he cannot be at
peace with himself nor with any of those around him.

Not only does Connolly suggest Brown's disillusionment,
but he argues that Brown's Calvinistic religion is a major
cause of his disillusionment.[9] Connolly presents this doctrine of Calvinism to his readers:

> Calvinism teaches that man is innately de-
> praved and that he can do nothing to merit

---

[8] Thomas E. Connolly, "Hawthorne's 'Young Goodman Brown':
An Attack on Puritanic Calvinism," _American Literature_, 28
(November, 1956), 372.

[9] Ibid., p. 375.

Format of the Research Paper

> salvation. He is saved only by the whim
> of God who selects some, through no de-
> serts of their own, for heaven while the
> great mass of mankind is destined for hell.[10]

I think Goodman Brown was a Calvinist, in the sense that he
believed himself to be one of God's Elect. I do not think,
however, that Brown found nothing to merit salvation, for
even though he believed himself to be one of the Elect, he
knew he must cling to his faith in order to get to heaven.
One particular group of Calvinists, known as Antinomians,[11]
were quite active during the time Hawthorne was writing "Young
Goodman Brown." It seems quite possible that this Calvinistic
group could have influenced Hawthorne's characterizations.
The Antinomians insisted that salvation was a function of
faith, for even a man's good works were secondary to his faith.
This "mysterious divine grace,"[12] as James W. Mathews calls it,
"was contingent on the degree of the individual's faith,"[13]
while a strong faith was a good indication of predestined
salvation. Extreme Antinomians believed that a man who was
of God's Elect could be confident of salvation, no matter
how the man conducted himself in his daily living. It seems
quite possible, then, that Brown could be classified as an
Antinomian, since he was depending on his faith to carry him

---

[10] Ibid., p. 374.

[11] James W. Mathews, "Antinomianism in 'Young Goodman
Brown,'" _Studies in Short Fiction_, 3 (Fall, 1965), 73-5.

[12] Mathews, p. 73.

[13] Ibid.

Model Research Paper

to heaven.

Mathews makes a strong case for Hawthorne's development of Antinomianism within young Goodman Brown. Brown himself does stress the theoretical rather than the practical side of his religion, as does the Antinomian doctrine. Brown states at one point in the story that "we are a people of prayer, and good works to boot, and abide no such wickedness."[14] Later in the story, Brown further adds, "With heaven above and Faith below, I will yet stand firm against the devil!" (p. 15). He is quite confident that his being one of God's Elect, along with his having Faith at home, will prevent any of the night's evil doings from becoming obstacles in his path to salvation.

It seems important at this point to look at Faith's relationship with her husband. Brown knows that his journey is of a sinful nature: "Poor little Faith! . . . What a wretch am I to leave her on such an errand!" (p. 10). Brown clearly manifests a sense of guilt for leaving his wife, because he seems to think it would "kill her" if she knew why he was going on his journey. However, I think Faith does know his purpose, because she says to her husband,

---

[14] This and subsequent quotations from the story "Young Goodman Brown" are taken from the text of the story as reprinted in Nathaniel Hawthorne: Young Goodman Brown, ed. Thomas E. Connolly (Columbus, Ohio: Charles E. Merrill Publishing Company, 1968), pp. 10-21. Hereafter, quotations from this version of the story will be documented with page-numbers in parentheses at the end of the quotation.

Format of the Research Paper

> "Dearest heart," whispered she, softly
> and rather sadly . . . "prithee put off
> your journey until sunrise and sleep in
> your own bed tonight. . . . Pray tarry
> with me this night, dear husband, of all
> nights in the year" (p. 10).

Why would Faith be <u>sad</u> to see her husband leave for just
one night, and why would she <u>beg</u> him to stay home on this
particular evening? Faith not only realizes her husband's
plans but even gives her consent and asks for God's blessing
to be with Brown when he insists that he must go: "'Then God
bless you!' said Faith, . . . 'and may you find all well
when you come back'" (p. 10). I think Faith is particularly
concerned with her husband's state of mind <u>after</u> the night's
experience. Faith does not appear extremely worried about
his leaving, but I think she doubts whether he can accept the
consequences. Faith's ability to see that her husband may
suffer from the results of his journey is Hawthorne's way of
subtly informing his readers that Faith is the wiser and the
more realistic of the two. She knows that her husband will
soon find out the hard way that Faith--both his wife <u>and</u> his
religion--cannot be used at his convenience whenever he is
troubled.

Connolly sheds an even brighter light upon young
Goodman Brown's faith. He points out that Brown did not
lose his faith at all. What Brown did do was not only retain his faith but actually discover "the full and frightening
significance of his faith."[15] Connolly illustrates his point

---

[15] Connolly, p. 371.

Model Research Paper

with this line from the story: "And when he had lived long,
and was borne to his grave a hoary corpse, followed by Faith,
an aged woman, and children and grandchildren, . . . they
carved no hopeful verse upon his tombstone, for his dying
hour was gloom" (p. 21). I must agree with Connolly that
Brown's faith--both his wife and his religion--did survive
him. Brown did not lose his wife, even though he did
lose the love and trust that had once linked them together
happily. And Brown did not lose his religion, for I feel
that when Hawthorne wrote this story, he knew that the
Calvinistic faith would outlive Goodman Brown. I think
Hawthorne realizes that many more "young Goodman Browns"
would perish as an indirect result of such a dehumanizing
religion.

Besides the subject of faith in "Young Goodman Brown,"
I would also like to touch upon the over-all implications of
the story. Without a doubt, ambiguity is quite prevalent
throughout the story. For example, one critic asked, "Does
the story have universal significance, or is it merely an
individual tragedy?"[16] Another critic questioned whether
young Goodman Brown represents the majority of the human
race or only a small segment of the human population.[17]
Various critics have asked similar questions and have

---

[16] Paul W. Miller, "Hawthorne's 'Young Goodman Brown':
Cynicism or Meliorism?" Nineteenth-Century Fiction, 14
(December, 1959), 255.

[17] Ibid.

Format of the Research Paper

arrived at a variety of answers.

Paul W. Miller is one critic who has struggled with
the question of whether Brown should be viewed as an individual or a type, representing either all of mankind or only
a segment of it. Miller seems to think that no conclusion
can be drawn concerning Brown's representation because the
answer depends on "one's understanding of Hawthorne's view
of man when he wrote the story, as well as one's interpretation of this enigmatic but nonetheless fascinating tale."[18]
Miller contends that if young Goodman Brown is intended to
represent all mankind, then Hawthorne must be regarded as
a totally cynical man; whereas if Brown represents only a
segment of mankind, then Hawthorne could be viewed less pes-
simistically. Miller brings up an interesting point here.
If Brown does not represent all mankind, are men like Brown
doomed by their nature alone to be separated from God, or
does the society in which they live play a major role in
separating them from God?[19] I think that, in Brown's case,
the society in which he lives has developed a religion that
refuses to acknowledge sin as an inevitable human weakness.
Man is responsible for his separation from God, but the
Calvinistic religion seems to suggest that a man's reunifi-
cation with God is unobtainable if he is not one of the

---

[18] Ibid.

[19] Miller, p. 256.

Model Research Paper

Elect. Human society ultimately strives to develop a religion to fill man's need for spiritual comfort, but it
appears that the Calvinists developed a religion that tor-
tured man's spirit. What portion of mankind, then, does
Brown represent? Miller contends that

> he represents those weaker members of a
> puritanical society who are traumatized,
> arrested in their spiritual development,
> and finally destroyed by the discovery
> that their society is full of "whited
> sepulchres."[20]

I find Miller's interpretation more acceptable than other
critics' views. Young Goodman Brown's spiritual development has been not only retarded but warped at the same time,
but I do not think Brown himself can be fully blamed.

I can agree only in part with D. M. McKeithan's opinion
about the over-all implication of the story.[21] He contends
that

> this is not a story of the disillusionment
> that comes to a person when he discovers
> that many supposedly religious and vir-
> tuous people are really sinful; it is,
> rather, a story of a man whose sin led
> him to consider all other people sinful.[22]

I think Brown is extremely disillusioned when he realizes the
sinful nature of Goody Cloyse, Deacon Gookin, and his own wife,
Faith. As I view the story, this disillusionment, which denies
all that Brown had previously believed, is a major factor in

---

[20] Ibid., p. 262.

[21] McKeithan, pp. 93-6.

[22] Ibid., pp. 95-6.

Format of the Research Paper

the over-all meaning of the story. Those persons who had
always seemed virtuous, pure, and representative of Brown's
religion were suddenly seen in a different light--a definite
disillusionment for young Goodman Brown. Contrary to
McKeithan's view, the story does seem to imply that Brown
is disillusioned when he discovers that certain virtuous
people are sinful and that Brown becomes painfully aware of
his own sinfulness and of the sinfulness of his fellowmen.
However, even with the disillusionment that Brown faces and
the realization of his own sinful nature, he still fails to
perceive two very important characteristics of sin: its
universal and inevitable nature.

I also agree, in part, with Herbert Schneider, who
places particular importance on Hawthorne's concern with
the sinful side of human nature. He writes of Hawthorne,

> For him sin is an obvious and conspicuous fact,
> to deny which is foolish. Its consequences
> are inevitable and to seek escape from them
> is childish. The only relief from sin comes
> from public confession. Anything private or
> concealed works internally until it destroys
> the sinner's soul.[23]

I strongly agree with Schneider that Hawthorne's denial of
sin is foolish and that its consequences are inevitable.
However, I question whether Hawthorne feels that a _public_
confession is the sole relief from sin. I think Hawthorne
would feel that a private confession could adequately render

---

[23] Herbert W. Schneider, _The Puritan Mind_ (New York:
H. Holt and Company, 1930), p. 260.

-11-

a sense of relief from one's sinfulness. Young Goodman Brown
was unable to bring himself to make either a public or a private confession. He could not accept the sin he saw in others
nor the sin present within himself, primarily because Calvinistic teachings failed to inform him that sin in man is inevitable. Paul Miller sums up my feelings quite well when
he says,

> In "Young Goodman Brown," then, Hawthorne
> . . . is pleading that what survives of
> Puritan rigorism in society be sloughed off
> and replaced by a striving for virtue start-
> ing from the confession of common human
> weakness. Such a society would be based
> upon the firm foundation of humility and
> honesty rather than the sinking sands of
> human pride and the hypocrisy that accom-
> panies it.[24]

I do agree with Miller that even a type like Brown could survive in a society like the one described above. Society can
truly have an adverse effect upon man, as did Goodman Brown's
society. But, at the same time, man must face the realities
of society, as Faith seemed to do, even though the pressures
of society oftentimes seem unbearable.

Doesn't it seem slightly odd that the mere actions of one
character could elicit so many interpretations from critics?
That there should be so many different interpretations seems
quite out of the ordinary to me. Yet when one considers the
questions that Nathaniel Hawthorne was dealing with in "Young
Goodman Brown," the ambiguity present in the story seems as

---

[24] Miller, p. 264.

Format of the Research Paper

inevitable as the sin that is present in man. In "Young
Goodman Brown," Hawthorne found himself dealing with the
mysteries about human nature and the human mind, two mysteries that naturally stimulate man to question. And this
questioning will go on forever, hopefully, because unless
man finds answers to questions concerning his spiritual
being or to questions concerning all the intricacies of
the human mind, life will hardly be worth living.

     I think Hawthorne truly valued this questioning when he
wrote this masterpiece. By his dealing with man's faith and
man's society, Hawthorne was able to stimulate man to question
his beliefs and his own personal role in society. Hawthorne
wanted to point out to the Calvinists in a subtle way that
their religious teachings were having an adverse effect upon
certain people. And I think he wanted the Calvinists to see
that the society--not the individual--needed the reform.
Through his characterization of Faith, Hawthorne was able to
show that man could be considered virtuous, even though he
is guilty of some degree of sin. And, finally, I think
Hawthorne wanted his readers to see that man's doubtfulness
concerning his salvation was <u>natural</u> and <u>necessary</u>, for if man
definitely knew that he was one of God's Elect, he would take
love and faith and peace of mind for granted. Young Goodman
Brown lost all doubt concerning his salvation for only one
night, but his experience on that one night caused Brown to
live the rest of his life as an extremely unhappy man.

BIBLIOGRAPHY

Connolly, Thomas E. "Hawthorne's 'Young Goodman Brown': An Attack on Puritanic Calvinism," <u>American Literature</u>, 28 (November, 1956), 370-5.

Fogle, Richard H. "Ambiguity and Clarity in Hawthorne's 'Young Goodman Brown,'" <u>New England Quarterly</u>, 18 (December, 1945), 448-465.

Hawthorne, Nathaniel. "Young Goodman Brown," <u>Nathaniel Hawthorne</u>: <u>Young Goodman Brown</u>, ed. Thomas E. Connolly. Columbus, Ohio: Charles E. Merrill Publishing Company, 1968, pp. 10-21.

McKeithan, D. M. "Hawthorne's 'Young Goodman Brown': An Interpretation," <u>Modern Language Notes</u>, 67 (February, 1952), 93-6.

Mathews, James W. "Antinomianism in 'Young Goodman Brown,'" <u>Studies in Short Fiction</u>, 3 (Fall, 1965), 73-5.

Miller, Paul W. "Hawthorne's 'Young Goodman Brown': Cynicism or Meliorism?" <u>Nineteenth-Century Fiction</u>, 14 (December, 1959), 255-264.

Schneider, Herbert W. <u>The Puritan Mind</u>. New York: Henry Holt and Company, 1930.

Walsh, Thomas F., Jr. "The Bedeviling of Young Goodman Brown," <u>Modern Language Quarterly</u>, 19 (December, 1958), 331-6.

Format of the Research Paper

(The bibliography for a paper submitted as a classroom assignment may be single-spaced, as it is in the model above. The bibliography for a paper submitted for publication, however, should be double-spaced, both within the entry and between entries, as in the Models for Bibliography [pp. 147–151]. Notice that the entries above are arranged in alphabetical order.)

(O)
Format of the Research Paper:
Model for Footnotes Entered on Separate Pages

(If footnotes are entered on separate pages at the end of a research paper submitted as a classroom assignment, they may be single-spaced within the footnote and double-spaced between footnotes, just as they are at the bottom of the page in the sample pages of the research paper. If a paper is submitted for publication, however, the footnotes must be entered on separate pages and must be double-spaced both within and between footnotes, as they are in the model below.)

[1]All my quotations from the "Elegy" are taken from the final approved version of 1753, as printed in Herbert W. Starr and John R. Hendrickson, eds., The Complete Poems of Thomas Gray, English, Latin, and Greek (Oxford: Clarendon Press, 1966). Hereafter, quotations from this edition of the poem will be documented by line numbers in parentheses.

Format of the Research Paper

[2]Samuel Johnson, "Gray," The Lives of the English Poets, ed. George Birkbeck Hill (Oxford: Clarendon Press, 1905), III, 442.

[3]Odell Shephard, "A Youth to Fortune and to Fame Unknown," Modern Philology, 20 (1923), 347-73.

[4]Ibid., p. 348.

[5]A detailed description of the various manuscript versions is given in Francis G. Stokes, ed., An Elegy Written in a Country Churchyard (Oxford: Clarendon Press, 1929), pp. 23-6. Herbert W. Starr has also presented an illuminating study of the successive versions of the poem in his article "Gray's Craftsmanship," JEGP, 45 (1946), 415-29.

[6]Shephard, p. 366.

[7]Ibid., pp. 371-2.

[8]H. W. Starr, "'A Youth to Fortune and to Fame Unknown': A Re-estimation," JEGP, 48 (1949), 97-107.

Forms For Letters

General Instructions

The one type of writing that most people engage in after they leave school is letter-writing. They will almost certainly write letters to parents, friends, and acquaintances; occasionally they may feel compelled to write a letter to the editor of a newspaper or magazine; and sometimes they may write more formal letters to institutions or officials for such purposes as applying for a job, requesting information or service, or seeking redress of some grievance. Although they do not have to be much concerned about the niceties of form when they are writing to intimate friends, they would be well advised to observe the conventions of form and etiquette in letters to people with whom they are not familiar enough to address them by their first name.

Letters written to acquaintances are commonly referred to as "familiar letters." Although "anything goes" in letters to acquaintances, one should keep in mind that even the most intimate acquaintance is flattered if the author of the letter observes certain amenities of form. A model for a familiar letter appears on p. 173. Here is a list of the conventions for the familiar letter:

Forms for Letters

(a) Familiar letters may be written on lined or unlined paper of any size, but usually they are written on note-size stationery of some pastel color.

(b) Familiar letters may be handwritten and may occupy both sides of the page.

(c) The writer puts his own address and the date at the right-hand side of the heading but does not, as in a business letter, put the name and address of the person to whom he is writing at the left-hand side of the heading.

(d) Depending on the degree of intimacy with the addressee, the writer can use salutations like these: **Dear Mom, Dear Jim, Dear Julie, Dear Ms. Worth.** The salutation is usually followed by a comma rather than the more formal colon.

(e) The body of the letter may be written in indented paragraphs, single- or double-spaced.

(f) Depending on the degree of intimacy with the addressee, the writer may use complimentary closes like these: **Much love, Affectionately, As ever, Cordially, Fondly.**

(g) Depending on the degree of intimacy with the addressee, the writer may sign his full name or just his first name or nickname.

Formal letters addressed to organizations or strangers or superiors are commonly called "business letters." The form of business letters is more strictly prescribed than that of familiar letters. Models for a business letter appear on pp. 174 and 177. Here is a list of the conventions for the business letter:

(a) Business letters are written on $8\frac{1}{2}$ x 11 unlined paper or on $8\frac{1}{2}$ x 11 paper with a printed letterhead.

(b) Business letters must be typewritten, on one side of the page only.

(c) In the sample business letter (p. 177) that is typed on printed letterhead stationery, another acceptable format for formal business letters is illustrated. Note that in this format, everything—date, address, greeting, text, salutation, etc.—begins at the left-hand margin. Compare this format with the format of the sample business letter (p. 174) that is typed on plain white paper. All the other directions about format (*d, e, f, g, h, i, j*) apply to both kinds of formal business letters.

(d) Flush with left-hand margin and in single-spaced block form, the writer should type the name and address of the person or the organization to whom he is writing. (This is the same form that will be used in addressing the envelope.)

(e) Two spaces below this inside address and flush with the left-hand margin, the writer should type the salutation, followed by a colon. If the writer is addressing an organization rather than a specific person in that organization, he can use salutations like **Dear Sir** or **Gentlemen** or **Dear Madam** or **Ladies.** If the writer knows the name of the person, he should use **Mr.** or **Miss** or **Mrs.** or, if uncertain about the marital status of a woman, **Ms.,** followed by the last name: **Dear Mr. Nelson, Dear Miss Kupferberg, Dear Mrs. Graham, Dear Ms. Bendo.** Women who feel that marital status should be no more specified in their own case than in that of a man (for whom **Mr.** serves, irrespective of whether he is married) prefer **Ms.** to **Mrs.** or **Miss. Messrs.** is the plural of **Mr.; Mmes.** is the plural of **Mrs.; Misses** is the plural of **Miss.** Professional titles may also be used in the salutation: **Dear Professor Buultjens, Dear Dr. Marton.** (*Webster's New Collegiate Dictionary* carries a list of the forms of address to various dignitaries [judges, clergymen, bishops, congressmen, etc.].)

Forms for Letters

(f) The body of the letter should be single-spaced, except for double-spacing between paragraphs. Paragraphs are not indented but start flush with the left-hand margin.

(g) The usual complimentary closes for business letters are these: **Yours truly, Very truly yours, Sincerely, Sincerely yours.** The complimentary close is followed by a comma.

(h) The writer should type his name about three or four spaces below the complimentary close. He should not preface his name with his professional title (e.g. **Dr., Rev.**) nor follow it with his degrees (e.g. **M.A., Ph.D.**), but below his typed name he may indicate his official capacity (e.g. **President, Director of Personnel, Managing Editor**). The writer should sign his name in the space left between the complimentary close and his typed name.

(i) If one or more copies of the letter are being sent to someone, that fact should be indicated with a notation like this in the lower left-hand side of the page (**cc.** is the abbreviation of **carbon copy**):

cc. Mary Hunter
    Robert Allison

(i) If the letter was dictated to, and typed by, a secretary, that fact should be indicated by a notation like this, flush with the left-hand margin and below the writer's signature (the writer's initials are given in capital letters, and the secretary's are given in lower-case letters): WLT/cs or WLT:cs.

See the following models for the text and envelope of a familiar letter and the two styles of business letters.

11 Silver Brook Rd.
Westport, CT 06880
January 5, 1977

Dear Christine,

I'm going back to school tomorrow, and since I didn't get a chance to call you, I thought I'd just write a note.

Did Mom tell you about my dorm's Solar Energy project? The solar collectors we built are in operation on the roof, helping to heat our dorm's water. We'll be calculating the energy savings to the University, and I'll write and tell you the results. New Hampshire winters <u>are</u> cold, but we think it'll work!

Love,
Julie

P.S. Say hi to Arthur!

Forms for Letters

239 Riverside Road
Columbus, OH 43210
January 5, 1977

Mr. Thomas J. Weiss
Manager, Survey Division
Acme Engineering Company, Inc.
5868 Fanshawe Drive
Omaha, NB 68131

Dear Mr. Weiss:

Mr. Robert Miller, sales representative of the Rushmore Caterpillar Company of Columbus and a long-time friend of my father, told me that when he saw you at a convention in Chicago recently, you indicated you would have two or three temporary positions open this summer in your division. Mr. Miller kindly offered to write you about me, but he urged me to write also.

By June, I will have completed my junior year in the department of Civil Engineering at Ohio State University. Not only do I need to work this summer to finance my final year of college, but I also need to get some practical experience in surveying on a large road-building project such as your company is now engaged in. After checking with several of the highway contractors in this area, I have learned that all of them have already hired their quota of engineering students for the summer.

For the last three summers, I have worked for the Worley Building Contractors of Columbus as a carpenter's helper and as a cement-finisher. Mr. Albert Michael, my foreman for the last three summers, has indicated that he would write a letter of reference for me, if you wanted one. He understands why I want to get some experience in surveying this summer, but he told me that I would have priority for a summertime job with Worley if I wanted it.

Among my instructors in civil engineering, the two men who know me best are Dr. Theodore Sloan, who says that he knows you, and Mr. A. M. Slater. Currently I have a 3.2 quality-point average in all my subjects, but I have straight A's in all my engineering courses. For the last two quarters I have worked as a lab assistant for Professor Sloan.

I am anxious to get experience in my future profession, and I am quite willing to relocate for the summer. I own a 1969 Volkswagen that I could use to commute several miles each day to the job site, if that is necessary. I am in good health, and I am willing to work very hard. If you want any letters of recommenda-

Forms for Letters

tion from any of the men named in my letter,
please let me know, but perhaps you will be
satisfied by Mr. Miller's testimony about me.

Sincerely yours,

Oscar Jerman

Oscar Jerman

c. Robert Miller

JOHN WILEY & SONS, INC., PUBLISHERS
605 THIRD AVENUE, NEW YORK, N.Y. 10016 (212) 867-9800

TELEX 12-7063   CABLE: JONWILE

January 5, 1977

Professor Edward P. J. Corbett
Department of English
The Ohio State University
Columbus, OH 43210

Dear Professor Corbett:

In reply to your query, I can say unequivocally that there are job
opportunities in the publishing industry for liberal-arts graduates
in general and for English majors in particular. In fact, for certain
kinds of jobs, the liberal-arts graduate would have a distinct advantage
over applicants with a more specialized training or education.

I am sure, however, that what your English majors are seeking is specific
information about the kinds of jobs available in publishing, about the
particular competencies and skills we look for in applicants, and about
the process of applying for jobs. I believe that I could offer this
information more clearly in an informal talk. It would also be more
convenient for me as daily office pressures allow little time for writing
the detailed report you need. You mentioned in your letter that the
English Forum regularly schedules a meeting for every third Friday of
the month. It happens that I am planning to visit your campus at a
time that coincides with the next scheduled meeting of that group.
I would be happy to address them and to attempt to answer questions.

If the English Forum is interested in meeting with me to find out about
job opportunities, it would be helpful if you would forward to me specific
questions that the students would like me to answer. I will, of course,
entertain other questions from the floor, but if I have a few questions
in advance, I will be better able to focus my talk.

I would also like to recommend a publication by The Modern Language
Association entitled English: The Pre-Professional Major. This brief
pamphlet by Linwood E. Orange should be read by English majors, prospective
English majors, and your faculty (if they do not already know it).
I think it is a very valuable guide to the employment potential of English
majors, and I recommend it highly.

Sincerely yours,

Thomas O. Gay
Editor

TOG/nb

cc: Mr. William Grant

NEW YORK LOS ANGELES SALT LAKE CITY LONDON SYDNEY TORONTO SOMERSET, N.J.

**Forms for Letters:
Models for Addressing
Envelopes (reduced size)**

FAMILIAR LETTER

Julie Worth
11 Silver Brook Rd
Westport, CT 06880

Ms. Christine Worth
331 Riverside Drive
New York, N. Y. 10025

BUSINESS LETTER

Mr. Oscar Jerman
239 Riverside Road
Columbus, OH 43210

Mr. Thomas J. Weiss
Manager, Survey Division
Acme Engineering Company, Inc.
5868 Fanshawe Drive
Omaha, NB 68131

Forms for Letters

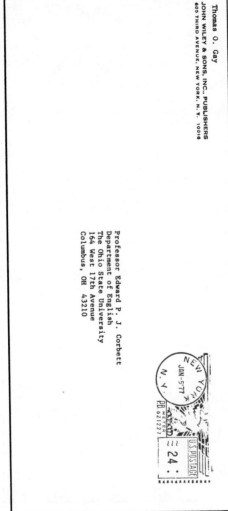

BUSINESS LETTER

Thomas O. Gay
JOHN WILEY & SONS, INC., PUBLISHERS
605 THIRD AVENUE, NEW YORK, N. Y. 10016

Professor Edward P. J. Corbett
Department of English
The Ohio State University
164 West 17th Avenue
Columbus, OH 43210

Two-Letter Abbreviations of States and Outlying Areas

Here is the U.S. Postal Service list of two-letter abbreviations of the fifty states, the District of Columbia, and outlying areas. These abbreviations should be set down in capital letters without a period and should be followed by the appropriate five-digit ZIP code—for example, Tempe, AZ 85281.

Alabama	AL	Illinois	IL
Alaska	AK	Indiana	IN
Arizona	AZ	Iowa	IA
Arkansas	AR	Kansas	KS
California	CA	Kentucky	KY
Colorado	CO	Louisiana	LA
Connecticut	CT	Maine	ME
Delaware	DE	Maryland	MD
District of Columbia	DC	Massachusetts	MA
Florida	FL	Michigan	MI
Georgia	GA	Minnesota	MN
Guam	GU	Mississippi	MS
Hawaii	HI	Missouri	MO
Idaho	ID	Montana	MT

Two-Letter Abbreviations of States and Areas

Nebraska	NB	Rhode Island	RI
Nevada	NV	South Carolina	SC
New Hampshire	NH	South Dakota	SD
New Jersey	NJ	Tennessee	TN
New Mexico	NM	Texas	TX
New York	NY	Utah	UT
North Carolina	NC	Vermont	VT
North Dakota	ND	Virgin Islands	VI
Ohio	OH	Virginia	VA
Oklahoma	OK	Washington	WA
Oregon	OR	West Virginia	WV
Pennsylvania	PA	Wisconsin	WI
Puerto Rico	PR	Wyoming	WY

Abbreviations of Place Designations in Addresses

(Note the absence of a period after these and in the two-letter abbreviations given above.)

Alley (Aly); Arcade (Arc); Avenue (Ave); Boulevard (Blvd); Branch (Br); Bypass (Byp); Causeway (Cswy); Center (Ctr); Circle (Cir); Court (Ct); Courts (Cts); Crescent (Cres); Drive (Dr); Expressway (Expy); Extended (Ext); Extension (Ext); Freeway (Fwy); Gardens (Gdns); Grove (Grv); Heights (Hts); Highway (Hwy); Lane (Ln); Manor (Mnr); Parkway (Pky); Place (Pl); Plaza (Plz); Point (Pt); Road (Rd); Rural (R); Square (Sq); Street (St); Terrace (Ter); Trail (Trl); Turnpike (Tpke); Viaduct (Via); Vista (Vis).

A Résumé

A résumé (pronounced *réz-oo-may*) is a one- or two-page summary, presented in the form of a list, of a job-applicant's life, relevant personal experiences, education, work experience, extracurricular activities, honors, goals, etc. It is usually submitted, along with such documents as academic transcripts, letter of reference, and specimens of one's writing, as part of a formal application for a job. The résumé is also referred to, and sometimes even labeled with, the Latin phrases *curriculum vitae* (the course of one's life) or *vita brevis* (a short life).

Under the headings of Education, Work Experience, and Extracurricular Activities, items are usually listed in a reverse chronological order, starting with the most recent and ending with the earliest. (See the sample résumé.)

A dossier (mentioned in the sample résumé) is a collection of one's documents (transcripts, letters of reference, etc.), which is kept on file in a school's placement office and which will be mailed out, upon request, to prospective employers. The letters of reference in a dossier are usually confidential—that is, they are letters written by teachers, employers, acquaintances and never seen by the applicant. (According to a federal law passed in 1975, however, applicants must be allowed to see any letters of reference about themselves if the letters were written after the law was passed and if the applicants have not signed a waiver to see the letters.) The names and addresses of other people who have agreed to write letters of reference upon request are often listed in the résumé as Additional References.

A Résumé

Depending upon the kind of job being applied for, some of the other categories that could be included in a résumé are Travel, Languages, Community Service, Research, Publications, Teaching Experience.

Résumé

Mary Watson Evans
239 E. Torrence Rd.
Columbus, OH 43214
Tel: (614) 267-4819 (home)
    (614) 422-6866 (office)

PERSONAL: Born, Milwaukee, Wisconsin, October 29, 1948

MARITAL STATUS: Married, James Evans, 1973; no children

EDUCATION: 1972-74, MBA (expected in June, 1974), Ohio State University, Columbus, OH
    Major--Accounting
1969-72, BA, Marquette University, Milwaukee, WI, graduated magna cum laude, 1972
    Major--Economics
    Minor--History
1966-69, Westside High School, Milwaukee, WI, graduated summa cum laude, 1969

WORK EXPERIENCE: Research assistant for Robert Moberly, Professor of Finance,
    Ohio State University, 1972-74
Check-out clerk, weekends and summers, A&P grocery store,
    Milwaukee, WI, 1971-72
Clerk-typist, summer of 1969, Allis Chalmers of Milwaukee
Clerk, Saturdays and summers, Gimbel's Department Store,
    Milwaukee, WI, 1967-68

EXTRA-CURRICULAR ACTIVITIES: Yearbook assistant editor, Marquette University, 1972
    Freshman representative on Student Council, Marquette
    University, 1969-70
    Reporter, Westside High School newspaper, 1967;
    editorial writer, 1968; editor, 1969

HONORS: $500 Scholarship from Rush Foundation, 1969-70
Full-tuition Scholarship from Omicron Society, 1971-72
Quill and Scroll award for Best Reporting, 1967

CAREER GOALS: Position as accountant or editor of in-house journal in a large
    accounting firm or bank in the Chicago area, where my husband,
    who will take his law degree in June, 1974, has accepted a position.
    I plan to take night courses in commercial law.

REFERENCES: My dossier is on file at the Placement Office, Ohio State University,
    164 W. 17th Avenue, Columbus, OH 43210

    Additional letters of reference (besides those in my dossier):

        Mr. John Anderson
        Personnel Manager
        Allis Chalmers Corporation
        West Allis, WI 53214

        Mr. Hans Schmitz
        Manager, A&P Stores (retired)
        2841 N. 70th Street
        Milwaukee, WI 53210

The Tenses of the English Verb

The following paradigms provide models for the tenses of regular verbs, irregular verbs, and the verb **to be** in Edited American English or in what this text calls "public prose."

Regular verbs are those that usually form the past tense by adding **-ed** to the present tense of the verb (e.g. **walk— walked**). A few regular verbs, however, simply add **-d** (e.g. **hope—hoped**) or **-t** (e.g. **deal—dealt**) to form the past tense; and some regular verbs double the final consonant (e.g. **hop—hopped**) or change the final **y** to **i** (e.g. **copy—copied**) before adding **-ed.**

Irregular verbs are those that form the past tense by some change of spelling *within* the verb (e.g. **run—ran; drink— drank; weave—wove**).

A good desk dictionary will indicate which of the regular verbs form the past tense in ways other than simply adding **-ed** and will give the present, the past, and often the past-participle forms of irregular verbs (e.g. **eat, ate, eaten**). Here is the beginning of a typical dictionary entry that lists, in order, the present tense, the past tense, the past participle, and the present participle of an irregular verb. If you are in doubt about any of the forms of an irregular verb, consult your dictionary.

The Tenses of the English Verb

drive (drīv) *vt.*.**drove, driv'en, driv'ing** [ME. *driven* < OE. *drifan,* akin to Goth. *dreiban,* G. *treiben,* ON. *drīfa* < IE. base **dhreibh-,* to push] **1.** to force to go; urge onward; push forward **2.** to force into or from a state or act [*driven* mad] **3.** to force to work, usually to excess **4.** *a*) to force by or as by a blow, thrust, or stroke *b*) to throw, hit, or cast hard and swiftly; specif., *Golf* to hit from the tee, usually with a driver **5.** to cause to go through; make penetrate **6.** to make or produce by penetrating [to *drive* a hole through metal] **7.** to control the movement or direct the course of (an automobile, horse and wagon, locomotive.)

With permission. From Webster's New World Dictionary of the American Language, *Second College Edition. Copyright © 1970 by the World Publishing Company, Inc.*

The Verb **To Be**

PRESENT TENSE	PAST TENSE	FUTURE TENSE
I **am** (cold)	I **was** (cold)	I **shall be** (cold)*
you **are**	you **were**	you **will be**
he/she/it **is**	he/she/it **was**	he/she/it **will be**
we **are** (cold)	we **were** (cold)	we **shall be** (cold)*
you **are**	you **were**	you **will be**
they **are**	they **were**	they **will be**

PERFECT TENSE	PAST PERFECT TENSE	FUTURE PERFECT TENSE
I **have been** (cold)	I **had been** (cold)	I **shall have been** (cold)*
you **have been**	you **had been**	you **will have been**
he/she/it **has been**	he/she/it **had been**	he/she/it **will have been**
we **have been** (cold)	we **had been** (cold)	we **shall have been** (cold)*
you **have been**	you **had been**	you **will have been**
they **have been**	they **had been**	they **will have been**

* Current usage also sanctions the use of **will** as the future-tense marker in the first person singular and plural.

The Tenses of the English Verb

ACTIVE VOICE

REGULAR VERBS

PRESENT TENSE
I **select** (the winner)
you **select**
he/she/it **selects**

we **select** (the winner)
you **select**
they **select**

PAST TENSE
I **selected** (the winner)
you **selected**
he/she/it **selected**

we **selected** (the winner)
you **selected**
they **selected**

FUTURE TENSE
I **shall select** (the winner)*
you **will select**
he/she/it **will select**

we **shall select** (the winner)*
you **will select**
they **will select**

IRREGULAR VERBS

PRESENT TENSE
I **drive** (the car)
you **drive**
he/she/it **drives**

we **drive** (the car)
you **drive**
they **drive**

PAST TENSE
I **drove** (the car)
you **drove**
he/she/it **drove**

we **drove** (the car)
you **drove**
they **drove**

FUTURE TENSE
I **shall drive** (the car)*
you **will drive**
he/she/it **will drive**

we **shall drive** (the car)*
you **will drive**
they **will drive**

The Tenses of the English Verb

PERFECT TENSE
I **have selected** (the winner)
you **have selected**
he/she/it **has selected**

we **have selected** (the winner)
you **have selected**
they **have selected**

PERFECT TENSE
I **have driven** (the car)
you **have driven**
he/she/it **has driven**

we **have driven** (the car)
you **have driven**
they **have driven**

PAST PERFECT TENSE
I **had selected** (the winner)
you **had selected**
he/she/it **had selected**

we **had selected** (the winner)
you **had selected**
they **had selected**

PAST PERFECT TENSE
I **had driven** (the car)
you **had driven**
he/she/it **had driven**

we **had driven** (the car)
you **had driven**
they **had driven**

FUTURE PERFECT TENSE
I **shall have selected** (the winner)*
you **will have selected**
he/she/it **will have selected**

we **shall have selected** (the winner)*
you **will have selected**
they **will have selected**

FUTURE PERFECT TENSE
I **shall have driven** (the car)*
you **will have driven**
he/she/it **will have driven**

we **shall have driven** (the car)*
you **will have driven**
they **will have driven**

The Tenses of the English Verb

PASSIVE VOICE

Only transitive verbs (that is, verbs that take a direct object—verbs listed in the dictionary as having **vt.** meanings) have a passive voice. An intransitive verb like *lie, lay, lain* can appear in all the tenses of the active voice, but because this verb cannot be followed by a direct object (one never says "he lies the book on the floor"), it cannot be turned into the passive voice.

REGULAR VERBS

PRESENT TENSE
I **am selected** (as the winner)
you **are selected**
he/she/it **is selected**

we **are selected** (as the winner)
you **are selected**
they **are selected**

PAST TENSE
I **was selected** (as the winner)
you **were selected**
he/she/it **was selected**

we **were selected** (as the winner)
you **were selected**
they **were selected**

IRREGULAR VERBS

PRESENT TENSE
I **am driven** (to school)
you **are driven**
he/she/it **is driven**

we **are driven** (to school)
you **are driven**
they **are driven**

PAST TENSE
I **was driven** (to school)
you **were driven**
he/she/it **was driven**

we **were driven** (to school)
you **were driven**
they **were driven**

The Tenses of the English Verb

FUTURE TENSE
I **shall be selected** (as the winner)*
you **will be selected**
he/she/it **will be selected**

we **shall be selected** (as the winner)*
you **will be selected**
they **will be selected**

PERFECT TENSE
I **have been selected** (as the winner)
you **have been selected**
he/she/it **has been selected**

we **have been selected** (as the winner)
you **have been selected**
they **have been selected**

PAST PERFECT TENSE
I **had been selected** (as the winner)
you **had been selected**
he/she/it **had been selected**

we **had been selected** (as the winner)
you **had been selected**
they **had been selected**

FUTURE TENSE
I **shall be driven** (to school)*
you **will be driven**
he/she/it **will be driven**

we **shall be driven** (to school)*
you **will be driven**
they **will be driven**

PERFECT TENSE
I **have been driven** (to school)
you **have been driven**
he/she/it **has been driven**

we **have been driven** (to school)
you **have been driven**
they **have been driven**

PAST PERFECT TENSE
I **had been driven** (to school)
you **had been driven**
he/she/it **had been driven**

we **had been driven** (to school)
you **had been driven**
they **had been driven**

The Tenses of the English Verb

FUTURE PERFECT TENSE

I **shall have been selected** (as the winner)*

you **will have been selected**

he/she/it **will have been selected**

we **shall have been selected** (as the winner)*

you **will have been selected**

they **will have been selected**

FUTURE PERFECT TENSE

I **shall have been driven** (to school)*

you **will have been driven**

he/she/it **will have been driven**

we **shall have been driven** (to school)*

you **will have been driven**

they **will have been driven**

Puzzlers

Each group of sentences shows various treatments of a common problem in phrasing. The letters appearing after the sentences allow you to record your preferred solution and then to compare this with the corresponding number in the KEY at the end of the exercise. Besides testing you, the puzzlers can show very plainly—although without explanation—the preferable way of handling some problems that occur in your writing.

Puzzlers

(1) You believed it to be him (a)
You believed it to be he. (b)

(2) The reason is because he's sick. (a)
The reason is that he's sick. (b)

(3) Let you and I do it together. (a)
Let you and me do it together. (b)
Let's you and I do it together. (c)
Let's you and me do it together. (d)

(4) We feed children who we think are hungry. (a)
We feed children whom we think are hungry. (b)

(5) I saw a young girl who I guessed to be Mary. (a)
I saw a young girl whom I guessed to be Mary. (b)

(6) The paintings were works by an imposter pretending to be he. (a)
The paintings were works by an imposter pretending to be him. (b)

(7) They should receive with open arms he who comes bearing gifts. (a)
They should receive with open arms him who comes bearing gifts. (b)

(8) His words seemed to imply that he agreed with her. (a)
His words seemed to infer that he agreed with her. (b)

(9) The distance between each post is six feet. (a)
The distance between posts is six feet. (b)

(10) People seem to have been shorter many years ago. (a)
People seemed to have been shorter many years ago. (b)

(11) He is one of the finest men that has ever lived. (a)
He is one of the finest men that have ever lived. (b)

(12) What provoke men's curiosity are mysteries. (a)
What provoke men's curiosity is mysteries. (b)
What provokes men's curiosity are mysteries. (c)
What provokes men's curiosity is mysteries. (d)

(13) Compromise will prevail; no one or no group will be the victor. (*a*)
Compromise will prevail; no one and no group will be the victor. (*b*)

(14) This copy is the best of any I have seen so far. (*a*)
This copy is the best of all I have seen so far. (*b*)

(15) To use a word of Lincoln's, . . . (*a*)
To use a word of Lincoln, . . . (*b*)

(16) Her apple pies are preferable to her custard pies. (*a*)
Her apple pies are preferable than her custard pies. (*b*)

(17) Nobody in their right minds would say such a thing. (*a*)
Nobody in their right mind would say such a thing. (*b*)
Nobody in his right mind would say such a thing. (*c*)

(18) She was very amused. (*a*)
She was very much amused. (*b*)

(19) He had hardly left the room than she got on the phone. (*a*)
He had hardly left the room when she got on the phone. (*b*)

(20) He has dozens of virtues, to which is added a certain pride. (*a*)
He has dozens of virtues, to which are added a certain pride. (*b*)

(1) *a*	(6) *b*	(11) *b*	(16) *a*
(2) *b*	(7) *b*	(12) *d*	(17) *c*
(3) *b*	(8) *a*	(13) *b*	(18) *b*
(4) *a*	(9) *b*	(14) *b*	(19) *b*
(5) *b*	(10) *a*	(15) *a*	(20) *a*

Glossary of Grammatical Terms

Some of these terms are defined in the section where they figure prominently. But since many of these terms also occur in other sections where they are not defined, this glossary is provided for the convenience of the curious but puzzled reader.

active verb. See **passive verb.**

adjective clause. An adjective clause is a dependent clause that modifies a noun or a pronoun, much as a simple adjective does.

The relative pronouns **who, which,** and **that** often appear at the head of the adjective clause, serving as the connecting link between the modified noun or pronoun and the clause, which then follows.

The car, **which was old and battered,** served us well.

Those are the houses **that I love best.**

Sometimes the relative pronoun is unexpressed but understood:

The book **I was reading** held my attention. (Here **that** is understood: The book **that** I was reading.)

See **dependent clause, relative pronoun, restrictive adjective clause, nonrestrictive adjective clause, modifier.**

Glossary of Grammatical Terms

adverb clause. An adverb clause is a dependent clause that modifies a verb or verbal, much as a simple adverb does.

The subordinating conjunction (**when, because, so that,** etc.), which appears at the head of the clause, links the adverb clause to the word that if modifies.

When I was ready, I took the examination.
I took the examination **because I was ready.**
To take an examination **when you are not ready** is dangerous.
(Here the adverb clause modifies the infinitive **to take.**)

See **dependent clause, subordinating conjunction, verbal, modifier.**

antecedent. An antecedent is the noun that a pronoun refers to or "stands for."

In the previous sentence, for example, the antecedent of the relative pronoun **that** is **noun.** In the sentence "The mother told her son that his check had arrived," **mother** is the antecedent of the pronoun **her,** and **son** is the antecedent of the pronoun **his.**

See **relative pronoun.**

auxiliary verbs. Auxiliary verbs are those function words—"helping" words (hence, "auxiliary")—that accompany other verb forms to indicate tense or mood or voice.

The following words in boldface are auxiliary verbs:
He **will** walk to work. He **is** walking to work. He **has** walked to work.
He **has been** walking to work. He **could** walk to work. He **must** walk to work.
He **was** driven to work.

See **function words, mood, voice.**

collective noun. A collective noun is a noun that desig-

Glossary of Grammatical Terms

nates a group or class of individuals—e.g. **committee, family, jury, army, faculty** (of a university), **team, crew.** See **summary noun.**

comma splice.   A comma splice is the use of a comma, instead of a coordinating conjunction or a semicolon, between the two independent clauses of a compound sentence.

> He could not tolerate noise, noise made him nervous and irritable.

Since the comma is a separating device rather than a joining device, it must be accompanied in this sentence by a coordinating conjunction (here **for**), or it must be replaced with a semicolon.

See **independent clause, compound sentence,** and **coordinating conjunction.**

complement.   A complement is the word or phrase, following a verb, that "completes" the predicate of a clause.

A complement may be (1) the object of a transitive verb (He hit **the ball**); (2) the noun or noun phrase following the verb **to be** (He is **an honors student**); or (3) the adjective following the verb **to be** or a linking verb (He is **happy**. The milk tastes **sour**.).

See **transitive verb, linking verb, to be, predicate complement,** and **noun phrase.**

complex sentence.   A complex sentence is one that consists of one independent clause and one or more dependent clauses.

The following complex sentence has two dependent clauses—the first one an adverb clause, the second an adjective clause:

> **When he got to the microphone,** he made a proposal **that won unanimous approval.**

Glossary of Grammatical Terms

As used by grammarians, the term has nothing to do with the length or complexity of the sentence.

    See **independent clause** and **dependent clause**.

compound sentence. A compound sentence is one that consists of two or more independent clauses.

    He was twenty-one, but she was only eighteen.
    Young men are idealists; old men are realists.

    See **independent clause** and **comma splice**.

compound word. A compound word is a combination of two or more words functioning as a single word.

    There are compounds that function as a noun (a **stand-in**), as an adjective (**eighteenth-century** literature), as a verb (they **pistol-whipped** him), or as an adverb (he had to comply **willy-nilly**). Some compounds have been used so often that they are written out with no space and no hyphen between the component parts (e.g. **handbook, postoffice**). Other compounds, especially those used as adjectives, are written with a hyphen (e.g. his **never-say-die** attitude). When in doubt about whether a compound should be hyphenated, consult a dictionary.

coordinate. Words, phrases, and clauses of the same grammatical kind or of equal rank are said to be "coordinate."

    A pair or series of nouns, for instance, would be a coordinate unit. An infinitive phrase yoked with a participial phrase would not be a coordinate unit, because the phrases are not of the same grammatical kind. An independent clause would not be coordinate with a dependent or subordinate clause, because the two clauses are not of equal rank. An alternative term for **coordinate** is **parallel**.

    See **parallelism** and **coordinating conjunction**.

Glossary of Grammatical Terms

coordinating conjunction. A coordinating conjunction is a word that joins words, phrases, or clauses of the same kind or rank. It joins nouns with nouns, verbs with verbs, prepositional phrases with prepositional phrases, independent clauses with independent clauses, adverb clauses with adverb clauses, etc.

A coordinating conjunction cannot be used to join a noun with an adjective, a prepositional phrase with a gerund phrase, or an independent clause with a dependent clause.

The coordinating conjunctions are **and, but, or, for, nor, yet, so.**

See **coordinate, correlative conjunctions,** and **subordinating conjunction.**

correlative conjunctions. Correlative conjunctions are coordinating conjunctions that operate in pairs to join coordinate structures in a sentence.

The common correlative conjunctions are **either . . . or, neither . . . nor, both . . . and, not only . . . but also,** and **whether . . . or.**

> By this act, he renounced **both** his citizenship **and** his civil rights.

See **coordinate** and **coordinating conjunction.**

dangling verbal. A dangling verbal is a participle, gerund, or infinitive (or a phrase formed with one of these verbals) that is either unattached to a noun or pronoun or attached to the wrong noun or pronoun.

> Raising his glass, a toast was proposed to the newlyweds by the bride's father.

In this sentence, the participial phrase **raising his glass** is attached to the wrong noun **(toast)** and therefore is said to be ''dangling'' (it was not the **toast** that was doing the **raising**). The participial phrase will be properly attached if

Glossary of Grammatical Terms

the noun **father** is made the subject of the sentence:
See **verbal** and **verbal phrase.**

demonstrative adjective. A demonstrative adjective is an adjective that ''points to'' its noun.

The singular forms are **this** (for closer objects—**this** book) and **that** (for more distant objects—**that** book); the plural forms are **these** and **those.**

dependent clause. A dependent clause is a group of words that has a subject and a finite verb but that is made part of, or dependent on, a larger structure by a relative pronoun **(who, which, that)** or by a subordinating conjunction (**when, if, because, although,** etc.).

There are three kinds of dependent clause: adjective clause, adverb clause, and noun clause.

A dependent clause cannot stand by itself; it must be joined to an independent clause to make it part of a complete sentence. A dependent clause written with an initial capital letter and with a period or question mark at the end of it is one of the structures that are called *sentence fragments.* An alternative term is **subordinate clause.**

See **independent clause, finite verb, adjective clause, adverb clause, noun clause, subordinating conjunction.**

finite verb. A finite verb is a verb that is fixed or limited, by its form, in person, number, and tense.

In the sentence ''The boy runs to school,'' the verb **runs** is fixed by its form in person (cf. **I run, you run**), in number (cf. **they run**), and in tense (cf. **he ran**). The verbals (participle, gerund, infinitive) are considered **infinite verbs** because although they are fixed by their form in regard to tense (present or past), they are not limited in person or number. The minimal units of a clause, whether it is de-

Glossary of Grammatical Terms

pendent or independent, are a subject (a noun phrase) and a finite verb:

> Bells ring. (but not: Bells ringing)

See **predicate verb, noun phrase, verbals.**

faulty predication. A faulty predication occurs when the verb or verb phrase of a clause does not fit semantically or syntactically with the subject or noun phrase of the clause. It results from the choice of incompatible words or structures.

> The shortage of funds **claimed** more money.
> The reason I couldn't go **was because I hadn't completed my homework.**

The verb **claimed** in the first sentence is semantically incompatible with the noun phrase **the shortage of funds** that serves as the subject of the clause. In the second sentence, the adverbial **because** clause is syntactically incompatible as a predicate complement following the verb **was.**

See **predicate complement, predicate verb, noun phrase, verb phrase.**

function words. Function words are those "little words" in the language that have very little vocabulary meaning but that perform such vital functions as connecting or relating other words in the sentence.

Sometimes called *particles,* function words comprise all such words in the language as the following:

(1) articles or determiners (in front of nouns): **the, a, an, this, that, these, those, all, some,** etc.

(2) prepositions (for connecting or relating their objects to some other word in the sentence): **of, from, above, on, at,** etc.

(3) coordinating conjunctions (for joining words, phrases, and clauses of equal rank): **and, but, or, for, nor, yet, so.**

Glossary of Grammatical Terms

(4) subordinating conjunctions (for joining clauses of unequal rank): **when, if, although, because, that,** etc.

(5) auxiliary verbs (for indicating changes in tense and mood): **will, shall, have, may, can, would, should,** etc.

(6) conjunctive adverbs (for providing logical links between clauses): **however, nevertheless, moreover, therefore,** etc.

(7) **not** with **do** or **does** or **did** (for negating a verb):

He **does not** love his mother.

He **did not** love his mother.

fused sentence. A fused sentence is the joining of two or more independent clauses without any punctuation or coordinating conjunction between them.

He could not believe his eyes mangled bodies were strewn all over the highway.

A fused sentence is also called a **run-on sentence** or a **run-together sentence.**

See **independent clause** and **comma splice.**

genitive case. The genitive case, a term derived from Latin grammar, is the case formed in English by adding **'s** or **s'** to the ending of nouns and some pronouns (e.g. **someone's**) or by using the preposition **of** followed by a noun or pronoun.

The most common use of the genitive case is to indicate possession: the **boy's** book, the arm **of the boy.**

Some of the other uses of the genitive case are as follows:

genitive of origin: **Beethoven's** symphonies

subjective genitive: the **king's** murder (i.e. the murder that the king committed)

objective genitive: the **king's** murder, the murder **of the king** (i.e. the king as the victim of a murder)

genitive of composition: a ring **of gold**

partitive genitive: a piece **of cheese**

Glossary of Grammatical Terms

The personal pronouns form the genitive case by a special spelling: **his, her, its, your, our, their.**

The genitive formed by adding **'s** or **s'** to nouns is often called the **possessive case.**

gerund. A gerund is a word that is formed from a verb but that functions as a noun.

Because of its hybrid nature as part verb and part noun, a gerund may take an object, may be modified by an adverb, and may serve in the sentence in any function that a noun can perform. Since, like the present participle, it is formed by adding **-ing** to the base verb, one can distinguish the gerund from the participle by noting whether it functions in the sentence as a noun rather than as an adjective. The following are examples of the gerund or gerund phrase performing various functions of the noun: As subject of the sentence: **Hiking** is his favorite exercise. As object of a verb: He favored **raising the funds by subscription.**

As complement of the verb **to be:** His most difficult task was **reading all the fine print.**

As object of preposition: After **reading the book,** he took the examination.

The latter sentence would be considered a dangling verbal if it were phrased as follows: After reading the book, the examination had to be taken.

See **verbal phrase** and **dangling verbal.**

independent clause. An independent clause is a group of words that has a subject and a finite verb and that is not made part of a larger structure by a relative pronoun or a subordinating conjunction.

The following group of words is an independent clause because it has a subject and a finite verb:

The **boys tossed** the ball.

The following group of words has the same subject and finite verb, but it is not an independent clause because it is made part of a larger structure by the subordinating conjunction **when:**

When the boys tossed the ball.

The **when** turns the clause into an adverb clause and thereby makes it part of a larger structure—a sentence consisting of a dependent clause (the adverb clause) and an independent clause (which must be supplied here to make a complete sentence).

See **dependent clause, finite verb, subordinating conjunction,** and **relative pronoun.**

infinitive. An infinitive is a word that is formed from a verb but that functions in the sentence as a noun or as an adjective or as an adverb.

Capable of functioning in these ways, the infinitive is more versatile than the participle, which functions only as an adjective, or the gerund, which functions only as a noun. The infinitive is formed by putting **to** in front of the base form of the verb.

Here are some examples of the infinitive or infinitive phrase in its various functions:

As noun (subject of sentence): **To err** is human; **to forgive** is divine.

As adjective (modifying a noun—in this case, **place**): He wanted a place **to store his furniture.**

As adverb (modifying a verb—in this case, **waved**): He waved a handkerchief **to gain her attention.**

The following infinitive phrase would be considered a dangling verbal:

To prevent infection, the finger should be thoroughly washed.

Glossary of Grammatical Terms

(Corrected: To prevent infection, you should wash the finger thoroughly.)

See **verbal phrase** and **dangling verbal.**

inflection. The inflection of a word is the change of form that it undergoes to show grammatical relation in its context or to express modification of its meaning.

The inflection of the verb *to be* appears in the entry **to be** below.

intransitive verb. An intransitive verb is a verb that expresses action but that does not take an object.

Intransitive verbs cannot be turned into the passive voice. Most action verbs in English have both transitive and intransitive uses, like **I ran swiftly** (intransitive) and **I ran the streetcar** (transitive). But some verbs can be used only transitively, like the verb *to emit,* and some verbs can be used only intransitively, like the verb *to go.* If in doubt about whether a particular verb can be used both transitively and intransitively, consult a dictionary.

The following verbs are all used intransitively:

He **swam** effortlessly.

They **slept** for twelve hours.

She **quarreled** with her neighbors.

See **transitive verb, passive verb,** and **voice.**

juncture. Juncture is a grammatical feature only of the spoken language. It concerns the ways in which we divide and articulate the stream of sound to make it intelligible to native speakers of the language.

There is the kind of juncture that operates within and between words to help us discriminate between spoken phrases like ''ice cream'' and ''I scream'' or between ''great rain'' and ''gray train.'' Another group of junctures makes use of various kinds of pauses or lengthening out of syllables to mark off the boundaries and terminations of utterances. This latter kind of juncture is roughly related to the punctuation system—commas, semicolons, periods, and question marks—of the written language.

linking verb. Linking verbs are those verbs of the senses like **feel, look, smell, taste, sound,** and a limited number of other verbs like **seem, remain, become, appear,** that "link" the subject of the sentence with a complement.

Linking verbs are followed by an adjective or a noun or a noun phrase:

The sweater **felt** soft. (adjective as complement)

He **appeared** calm. (adjective as complement)

He **remains** the president of the union (noun phrase as complement)

See **to be, complement, predicate complement,** and **noun phrase.**

modifier. A modifier is a word, phrase, or clause that limits, specifies, qualifies, or describes another word.

In the phrase "the red barn," the adjectival modifier **red** helps to specify or describe the particular barn being talked about. In the phrase "ran swiftly," the adverbial modifier **swiftly** describes the manner in which the action designated in the verb **ran** was done. Phrases and clauses also modify nouns and verbs:

the girl **with the flowery hat** (prepositional phrase modifying **girl**)

the barn **that is painted red** (adjective clause modifying **barn**)

he ran **down the street** (prepositional phrase modifying ran)

he ran **because he was frightened** (adverb clause modifying **ran**)

Glossary of Grammatical Terms

Besides modifying verbs, adverbs also modify adjectives and other adverbs:

It was an **unusually** brilliant color. (modifying the adjective **brilliant**)

He ran **very** swiftly. (modifying the adverb **swiftly**)

See **adjective clause, adverb clause,** and **squinting modifier.**

mood. Mood is that aspect of a verb which indicates the speaker's attitude toward the expressed action or condition. The **indicative mood** is used for statements of fact (The report **is** true); the **imperative mood** is used for commands (**Be** still!); the **subjunctive mood** is used to indicate hope or desire (I pray that they **be** happy), possibility (If it **be** true . . .), or condition (If he **were** here . . .). Except for the verb **to be,** the subjunctive forms of verbs are identical with the indicative forms except in the third-person singular of the present tense—e.g. **if he go** instead of **if he goes.**

nominative case. The nominative case is the form that a noun or pronoun must take when it appears as the subject of a clause or as the complement of a linking verb or of the verb **to be.**

In modern English, however, a writer has to be concerned about the nominative form only of some pronouns, because now nouns change their form only in the possessive case **(boy's, boys')** and in the plural **(boy, boys; man, men)**. The personal pronouns, however, and the relative pronoun **who** are still inflected (e.g. **he, his, him; who, whose, whom**). The nominative case of the personal pronouns are as follows: **I, you, he, she, it, we, they.**

The wrong case (the objective or accusative case) of the pronoun is used in this sentence:

Me hate the smell of burning rubber.

See **complement** and **inflection.**

nonrestrictive adjective clause. A nonrestrictive adjective clause is an adjective clause that supplies information about the noun or pronoun that it modifies but information that is not needed to identify or specify the particular noun or pronoun being talked about.

My father, **who is a college graduate,** cannot get a job.

In this sentence, the adjective clause **who is a college graduate** supplies information about the father, but that information is not needed to identify which father is being talked about. The particular father being talked about is sufficiently identified by the **my.**

A nonrestrictive adjective clause must be separated with a comma from the noun or pronoun that it modifies.

See **adjective clause, restrictive adjective clause,** and **modifier.**

noun clause. A noun clause is a dependent clause that can serve almost every function that a noun or pronoun or noun phrase can serve: as subject of the sentence, as an appositive to a noun, as the complement for a verb, as object of a preposition, but not as an indirect object.

The subordinating conjunctions that most often introduce a noun clause are **that** and **whether**—although **that** is sometimes omitted when the noun clause serves as the object of a transitive verb.

That he would make the grade was evident to everyone. (subject of sentence)

He said **he would not come.** (object of verb; **that** is omitted here, but it is just as correct to say **that he would come**)

The fact **that I had been sick** did not influence their decision.

Glossary of Grammatical Terms

(in apposition to **fact**)

They asked me about **whether I had seen him recently**. (object of the preposition **about**)

See **dependent clause, noun phrase,** and **complement.**

noun phrase. A noun phrase consists of a noun or a pronoun and all of its modifiers (if any).

In the following sentence all of the words in boldface would be considered part of the noun phrase, which is dominated by the noun **house:**

The big, rambling, clapboard house on the hill belongs to Mrs. Adams.

See **verb phrase** and **verbal phrase.**

parallelism. Parallelism is the grammatical principle that words, phrases, or clauses joined in a pair or in a series must be of the same kind.

Nouns must be coupled with nouns; prepositional phrases must be coupled with prepositional phrases; adjective clauses must be coupled with adjective clauses.

Parallelism breaks down, for instance, when a noun is yoked with an adjective or a prepositional phrase is yoked with a participial phrase. Parallelism has been preserved in the following sentence, because all the words in the series that serves as the predicate complement of the verb **was** are adjectives:

The engine was **compact, durable,** and **efficient.**

See **coordinate** and **coordinating conjunction.**

participle. A participle is a word that is formed from a verb but that functions as an adjective.

Because of its hybrid nature as part verb and part adjective, a participle may take an object, may be modified by an adverb, and may modify a noun or a pronoun.

Pulling his gun quickly from his holster, the sheriff fired a shot before the burglar could jump him.

In that sentence, the participle **pulling** takes an object **(gun)**, is modified by the adverb **quickly** and by the prepositional phrase **from his holster,** and modifies the noun **sheriff.**

The **present participle** is formed by adding **-ing** to the base form of the verb: **pulling, jumping, being.**

The **past participle** is formed by adding **-ed** or **-en** to the base form of the verb or by a special spelling: **pulled, beaten, left, bought.**

The **perfect participle** is formed with **having** plus the past participle form: **having pulled, having beaten, having left.**

The **passive participle** is formed with **having** plus **been** plus the past participle form: **having been pulled, having been beaten, having been left.**

See **verbal phrase** and **dangling verbal.**

passive verb. A passive verb is the form that a predicate verb takes when we want to indicate that the subject of the sentence is the receiver, not the doer, of the action.

The form that we use when we want to indicate that the subject is the doer of the action is called the **active verb.**

Only transitive verbs can be turned into the passive form. The passive verb is made by using some form of the verb **to be** (e.g. **am, is, are, was, were, has been**) and the past participle of the base verb.

The shepherds **tend** the sheep. (active verb)
The sheep **are tended** by the shepherds. (passive verb)

See **predicate verb, transitive verb, past participle, to be.**

possessive case. See **genitive case.**

Glossary of Grammatical Terms

predicate complement. Some grammarians use the term **predicate complement** to refer to any noun, pronoun, or adjective that follows, or "completes," the verb, whether it be a transitive verb, a linking verb, or the verb **to be.** Other grammarians use the term **object** for the noun or pronoun that follows a transitive verb and reserve the term **predicate complement** for the noun, pronoun, or adjective that follows a linking verb or the verb **to be.**

> He is the **president.** (noun following the verb **to be**)
> She became the **breadwinner.** (noun following the linking verb)
> The pie tastes **good.** (adjective following the linking verb)
> See **complement, transitive verb, linking verb, to be.**

predicate verb. A predicate verb is the finite-verb part of the verb phrase that constitutes the whole predicate of a dependent or independent clause.

> In the following sentence, the word in boldface is the predicate verb of the independent clause:
> The man **guided** the dogsled through the blinding snowstorm.
> See **finite verb** and **verb phrase.**

relative pronoun. The relative pronouns **who, which, that** serve a grammatical function in an adjective clause (as subject of the clause, as object or predicate complement of the verb of the clause, as object of a preposition in the clause) and also as the connecting link between the adjective clause and the noun or pronoun that the clause modifies.

> **Who** is the only one of these relative pronouns that is inflected: **who** (nominative case), **whose** (possessive case), **whom** (objective case).
> See **dependent clause, adjective clause,** and **antecedent.**

Glossary of Grammatical Terms

restrictive adjective clause. A restrictive adjective clause is an adjective clause that identifies or specifies the noun or pronoun that it modifies, that "restricts" the meaning to a particular person, place, thing, or idea.

> Baseball players who are under contract to a duly franchised professional team are eligible for a pension.

In this sentence, the adjective clause **who are under contract to . . . team** specifies those baseball players who are eligible for a pension. If that adjective clause were enclosed with commas (that is, if it were a **nonrestrictive** clause), the sentence would mean that *all* baseball players are eligible *because* they are under contract to a professional team—a quite different meaning from the sentence that does not have commas enclosing the adjective clause.

A restrictive adjective clause should *not* be separated with a comma from the noun or pronoun that it modifies.

See **adjective clause, nonrestrictive clause,** and **modifier.**

run-on sentence. See **fused sentence.**

sentence fragment. See **independent clause, dependent clause,** and **finite verb.**

squinting modifier. A "squinting modifier" is a metaphorical way of referring to an adverb or an adverbial phrase that is placed between two words that it can modify. Because by position it "looks both ways," it results in an ambiguous sentence.

For example: The candidate whom we favored **enthusiastically** praised our platform.

Since the adverb **enthusiastically** occupies a position between two verbs that it can modify (**favored** and **praised**), we cannot be sure whether it was the favoring or the praising that was done with enthusiasm. Shifting the

Glossary of Grammatical Terms

adverb to a position before **favored** or after **platform** will relieve the ambiguity.

See **modifier**.

subordinating conjunction. A subordinating conjunction is a word that serves as the connecting link between an adverb clause or a noun clause and a word in some other structure.

The most common subordinating conjunctions that connect an adverb clause to the verb or verbal that the clause modifies are **when, whenever, because, since, although, though, while, as, after, before, unless, until, in order that, so that.**

The two subordinating conjunctions that serve as the link between the noun clause and another structure are **that** and **whether.** The conjunction **that** is often omitted when the noun clause functions as the object of a verb:

He said [that] the committee would not accept the proposal.

See **coordinating conjunction, adverb clause, noun clause.**

summary noun. A summary noun is a word that "sums up" an idea or set of particulars presented in the previous sentence. It is usually accompanied by one of the demonstrative adjectives **this, that, these, those.**

He answered telephones, stuffed envelopes, rang doorbells, collected money, and distributed literature. This **work** [or These **activities**] won him a secure position on the candidate's campaign staff.

To avoid the vagueness or ambiguity of reference that may result from beginning a sentence with only a **this** or a **these,** the writer should use a summary noun along with **this** or **these** (or **that, those**).

See **collective noun** and **demonstrative adjective.**

Glossary of Grammatical Terms

suspended structure. A suspended structure is a phrase whose completion is delayed by an intervening parallel phrase. Both phrases are completed by a common element.

> His financial status is related to, and bolstered by, the vigor of the stock market.
>
> Weren't you at all fond of, or in the least bit in sympathy with, my stand on this issue?
>
> Employers are interested in the long-term, as well as the short-term, worth of our graduates.

A comma is usually put at the end of the first arrested phrase in order to signal to the reader that the phrase will be completed later in the sentence. This punctuation represents an exception to the rule stated in **62** that pairs of words, phrases, and dependent clauses joined by one of the coordinating conjunctions should not be separated with a comma.

terminal punctuation. Terminal punctuation is the period or question mark placed after a string of words to signal the end of a sentence or utterance.

Commas, semicolons, and colons—sometimes called **internal punctuation**—are used to mark the boundaries of phrases and clauses within the sentence. An alternative term for **terminal punctuation** is **end punctuation.**

to be. **To be** is the infinitive form of the most frequently used verb in the English language, one that can be followed by a noun, a pronoun, an adjective, an adverb of place (e.g. **there, here, upstairs**), the preposition **like** plus the object of that preposition (e.g. He is **like his father**), a verbal or verbal phrase, or a noun clause.

Here are the various forms of **to be,** as it changes in number, person, and tense: **am, is, are, was, were, shall**

Glossary of Grammatical Terms

be, will be, has been, have been, had been, shall have been, will have been.

Some form of **to be** along with the present participle of the base verb is also used to form the progressive tense of the English verb: He **was going** to the doctor regularly. He **had been going** to the doctor regularly.

Some form of **to be** along with the past participle of the base verb is also used to form a passive verb: He **was struck** on the head. He **has been struck** on the head.

See **linking verb, predicate complement, passive verb,** and **participle.**

transitive verb. A transitive verb is a verb expressing action that terminates in, or is received by, an object.

The object of a transitive verb can be a noun or noun phrase, a pronoun, a verbal or verbal phrase, or a noun clause.

> They **destroyed** the village. (noun as object)
> They **shot** him. (pronoun as object)
> He **favors** giving me another chance. (gerund phrase as object)
> He **will try** to break the lock. (infinitive phrase as object)
> He **proposed** that everyone in the room be allowed to vote. (noun clause as object)

Only transitive verbs can be turned into a passive verb.

See **intransitive verb** and **passive verb.**

verb phrase. A verb phrase is a group of words consisting of a verb and all of its auxiliaries (if any), all of its complements (if any), and all of its modifiers (if any).

In the following sentence, all words in boldface would be considered part of the verb phrase (a structure dominated by the verb):

> The army **has been severely restricted in its operations.**

Glossary of Grammatical Terms

See **noun phrase, verbal phrase, predicate verb, auxiliary verb, modifier.**

verbal. A verbal is the general name applied to participles, gerunds, and infinitives.

These words are called "verbals" because they are formed from verbs; because they are not finite verbs, they cannot by themselves serve as the predicate verb of an independent clause or a dependent clause.

See **participle, gerund, infinitive, finite verb, predicate verb.**

verbal phrase. A verbal phrase is a group of words consisting of a participle or a gerund or an infinitive and all of its complements (if any) and all of its modifiers (if any).

In the following sentence, all words in boldface would be considered part of the verbal phrase, which is dominated by the participle **leaving:**

Leaving behind all of its heavy equipment, the army pressed forward quickly.

voice. Voice is that aspect of a verb which shows the relation of the subject to the action, i.e. whether that of performer or recipient. The former is called **active voice** (I was loving), the latter **passive voice** (I was loved).

See **passive verb.**

Commonly Misspelled Words

accept (cf. except)
accidentally
acquire
acquaintance
address
all right
already (cf. all ready)
arithmetic
athletics
attendance

believe
benign
business

cemetery
changeable
chief
choose (cf. chose)
conscience
correspondent
definite

dependent
design
devise (cf. device)
diminution
disappearance
dispel

effect (cf. affect)
embarrass
environment
exaggerate
existence

familiar
fascinate
flagrant
foreign
forth (cf. fourth)
fragrant
friend
fulfill or fulfil
    (but not *fullfill*)

Commonly Misspelled Words

government

harass
height
hindrance

incredible
independent
irresistible
its (cf. it's)

judgment

library
literature
lose (cf. loose)

maintenance (cf. maintain)
mathematics
minuscule
miracle
miscellaneous
mischief

necessary
neighbor
noticeable
nuisance

occasion
occurrence
occurred
offered
omitted

parallel
peculiar

possess
preceding (cf. proceeding)
preferred
prejudice
principal (cf. principle)
privilege

quite (cf. quiet)

receive
referring
relieve
remuneration
resemblance
reverence
ridiculous

seize
separate
similar
special
stationary (immobile)
stationery (paper)
succeed

than (cf. then)
their (cf. there)
threshold
too (cf. to)
tragedy
truly

usually

whose (cf. who's)
withhold

Index

Index

Index